MAKE THE GRADE

First published in 2013 by Zest Books
35 Stillman Street, Suite 121, San Francisco, CA 94107
www.zestbooks.net

Text © 2013 by Lesley Schwartz Martin
Illustrations © 2007 by Michael Wertz
Page 90 to page 102 reproduced in part from *Where's My Stuff?*
by Samantha Moss with Lesley Schwartz © 2007 by Zest Books

Teen Nonfiction / School & Education
Library of Congress Control Number: 2012943317
ISBN: 978-1-936976-38-6

Cover design: Maija Tollefson
Book design: Marissa Feind

Manufactured in China
SCP 10 9 8 7 6 5 4 3 2 1
4500403251

Connect with Zest!
zestbooks.net/blog
zestbooks.net/contests
twitter.com/ZestBooks
facebook.com/ZestBook
facebook.com/BookswithaTwist
pinterest.com/ZestBooks

MAKE THE GRADE

EVERYTHING YOU NEED TO STUDY BETTER, STRESS LESS, AND SUCCEED IN SCHOOL

LESLEY SCHWARTZ MARTIN

TABLE OF CONTENTS

Introduction

Everyone acknowledges how important a quality education is for both personal and professional success. But that basic reality doesn't alter the fact that learning can be kind of a bummer. Turning down a night out with friends to study? Disappointing. Skipping Thursday night comedies because you have to read *Romeo and Juliet?* Frustrating. And dance lessons in Gym class? Downright ridiculous.

There are some things about school—homework, for instance, and cafeteria lunches, and early morning commutes—that you just have to put up with; but stress, anxiety, and disappointing grades aren't among them. Those are the things that you can cut out of your school life, and *Make the Grade* will show you how.

Make the Grade is intended as a comprehensive guide to studying better and stressing less—and as a result, we've covered a huge array of problems and issues here. Do you have a tendency to forget your homework assignments? Open up to chapter seven, and learn how to put together a study group that you can really rely on. Do you study in bed, with the TV on and your iPhone within arm's reach? Probably not the best idea. In chapter three, we'll go over some simple measures you can take to stay focused. Or maybe you're getting the distinct impression that a certain teacher hates you? Well, you might want to consider asking for a seat assignment that's not next to your best friend. (More on that in chapter five.)

School can be rough, but if it weren't a challenge then it wouldn't be very interesting, either. *Make the Grade* offers dozens of simple changes you can make in order to transform the way you approach school, homework, studying, and (or course) the all-important tests. Setting goals, making a schedule, and improving relationships with teachers can all have a major impact on your overall success. And it's not just about grades—it's also about developing habits that will set you up for success in your life outside of school as well.

School shouldn't be just about surviving, it should also be about having a great time, and setting yourself up for the life you want to live when school is over. And whether you're looking for guidance in a particular class, or hoping to make a fresh start in a new school year, *Make the Grade* is here to help.

Part 1

A Roadmap to Success

Successful students don't get good grades because they're smarter than everyone else. Smarts helps, of course, but students do well because they can map out what matters most to them, and then follow through, putting maximum effort in where necessary, and not wasting valuable time on things that are less important.

The great thing is that these prioritizing techniques are available to everyone, and if you adopt them, you'll not only do better in school but also learn great skills you can use in applying for jobs, getting into college, and even navigating personal relationships as well.

With the advice in Part 1, you'll soon be mapping out smart and realistic goals, putting together a weekly schedule to help maximize every hour of your day, tracking your homework and your life in a way that helps you get everything done on time, and finding ways to get engaged in school even when things get—what's the word?—oh yeah: boring.

Chapter 1
Setting Meaningful Goals

As you move from middle school to high school to college, it's important to remember that *your* life is *your* life. Your parents helped to shape your identity while you were growing up—they're the ones who brought you out here, after all—but now it's not up to them to decide what you'll do and how you'll do it. As you grow older, the responsibility for big life decisions rests more and more on your shoulders.

You have the power to shape your own life, and the earlier you can take ownership of that, the better. Setting goals is a great way to gain a greater sense of control over your life and get moving in a positive direction. And research shows that setting goals enhances students' overall experience in high school, in addition to improving academic performance.

WHAT LIGHTS YOUR FIRE?

At the beginning of every school year you should take a few minutes to write out your goals. And keep an open mind about what your goals can include! They can be about grades ("I want a B+ average"), achievements ("I want to make the varsity swimming team"), or feelings ("I want to be less stressed"). If it matters to you, it's fair game. They're your goals, after all!

Then, once you've decided which goals you're really going to prioritize and pursue, put that list somewhere where you can see it every day. That way, when you start to feel discouraged, you can easily remind yourself of some of the reasons why you should keep going.

We'll assume that "success in school" is near the top of your list of goals, but that still leaves some key questions open, like what success means for you, and how you—with your own specific set of studying skills and studying shortcomings—can do your very best. These are complicated questions, and time is of the essence, so let's get to it!

Setting Goals: Getting There Step by Step

Goals come in all shapes and sizes. Long-term goals relate to dreams you have for the future, like where you want to go to college, or what kind of career you want to have. The best way to reach those bigger goals is to set short-term goals. Short-term goals are the small steps you take every day, and that collectively keep you on pace to achieve those longer-term goals. Reaching smaller milestones also feels great, helping to keep you motivated, and showing how much progress you're making along the way!

Lots of incredibly successful people point to short-term goals as a key component in their development. As Michael Jordan wrote in his book *I Can't Accept Not Trying*, "As I look back, each one of the steps or successes led to the next one. When I got cut from the varsity team as a sophomore in high school, I learned something. I knew I never wanted to feel that bad again... So I set a goal of becoming a starter on the varsity... When it happened, I set another goal... I gained a little confidence every time I came through." (And in case you weren't already aware, Michael Jordan wound up having a pretty good basketball career in the end.)

Like Michael Jordan said, when you're making progress, you feel more confident and it's easier to keep going, but if you feel like you're not getting anywhere, it's easy to get bummed out.

YOUR GOALS SHOULD BE *YOUR* GOALS

When creating goals, make sure that they're what you really want for yourself and what you believe you can actually achieve. It's all too easy to let parents, friends, coaches, and teachers influence you. But at the end of the day, *you're* the one who has to accomplish these goals. If you're trying to impress somebody else, chances are you'll get off track or lose motivation.

Making SMART Goals

Imagine trying to run a race where there was no course or finish line. It wouldn't work out very well. You would have no sense of where you needed to run, or how fast, and you wouldn't even be able to tell when the race had ended!

Goals need a finish line, too. And that's where SMART goals come in.

SMART goals are Specific, Measurable, Achievable, Relevant, and Time-based. Let's break them down:

Specific

If you want to set yourself up for success, your goals need to be specific. Goals are often too vague or loose, making it hard to know if you have actually achieved anything. Saying "I want to improve my grades" is an admirable dream, but it's also pretty vague, whereas "I want to start getting at least 9/10 on the weekly geometry quiz" gives you a very definite bar to clear. There will be no doubt when you get there.

Measurable

Goals that are measurable allow you to easily figure out if you are getting closer to your target. Measurable goals involve things like percentages, days, weeks, or times. "I want to get over 80% on the next four biology quizzes" is a clear and concrete goal—and once it's achieved, you can start shooting for 85% . . . then 90% . . . and then for straight A's!

Achievable

If you have a C average in a class and you only have four weeks left in the semester, trying to get an A for your final grade might be unrealistic. And if you don't think you can really achieve it, then you probably won't be motivated to try. It's super important to set goals that make you push yourself but are also within your reach. Figure out what you can achieve given your skills, and how much time and energy you can commit before you set your goals.

Relevant

Set goals that are important to you. Do you really have the desire to achieve the goal you've set for yourself? On a scale of 1 to 10 (10 being the highest), how committed are you to achieving this goal? If the answer is less than an 8, you might want to adjust the goal and make it more aligned with what matters to you most. Whatever goal you set, make sure it fits in with the other things you are trying to achieve.

Time-based

Finally, your goal needs to be time-based. Give yourself a deadline for completion so that you can create a sense of urgency for yourself. This will also help you keep track of your progress.

Get on the Road to Your Goals

Setting goals is great, but eventually you need to get started (which is often the hardest part). It's easier to build momentum when you plan out the first few things you are going to do. And don't forget the details: Make sure your plan provides a clear sense of who, what, when, where, and how. So let's say your goal is to complete 100 note cards for your research paper by next Friday. If we break that down, here's what it looks like.

Who

You. But who knows, you might need to hit up someone else—a friend or sibling maybe—for a ride to the library to pick up books.

What

You've got that one figured out—100 note cards.

When

Doing 100 note cards all at once seems a bit much. Let's break up the work. Spend Sunday at the library from 1:00 to 2:00 pm to pick up books, and Monday, Wednesday, and Friday from 5:00 to 6:00 pm to write up the notes.

Where

Research at the library, then make the note cards at home at your desk.

How

Write up 35 note cards on Monday, 35 on Wednesday, and 30 on Friday. Use the handout from class to guide the formatting.

Tips for Achieving Your Goals

There are lots of tricks that help us to remember and stay on top of our goals. Here are a few ways to stay on track.

Write It Down (And Put it Somewhere You Can See It)

Researchers say that when we write things down, we become more committed to them. You're also more likely to remember things better when you write them down. So, as you come up with goals for yourself, pull out some notebook paper, open up a Word doc, or make a recording on your smartphone. You can always go back and change your list, but take the time to record your thoughts—and then after you've made your list, be sure to put it somewhere you can see it! The more frequently you encounter your goals, and the more often you think about them, the more real they'll become. Before you know it, that list will become a reality.

CHANGING YOUR HABITS

To actually stick to your goals, you might have to change your habits . . . which can have you pulling your hair out until those habits become second nature. But stick with it! For example, if you're trying to write down your assignments every day during class rather than after school all at once, it might take a few weeks for you to retrain your brain and make that a routine. Just like other muscles in your body, the brain needs some time to get in shape and develop muscle memory. Give yourself a month of doing something every day to make it a new habit.

Tell a Friend

Are you the kind of person who tells your friends *everything*? Here's a way you can spin that to your advantage. Some people find it motivating to tell other people about their goals. Whether it's because saying it out loud makes it seem more real, or because your friends tease you if you're not sticking with it, sharing your goal with someone else can make you more committed to it. If you tell your best friend that you're applying for a scholarship, she'll probably bring it up and ask how it's going. You aren't going to want to disappoint either yourself or her.

Picture It

What better way to work for success than to have a visual reminder? Pick a photo, create a collage, or draw something that represents that long-term goal of yours. It could be a brochure for the college you want to attend, an ad for the car you're saving up for, or maybe a flyer for a play you want to direct. Try it out!

Break It Down

When a goal seems too big, break it down into smaller pieces so that you can see how you're doing. Say, for example, you are writing a research paper. Ultimately you will need to turn in five to seven double-spaced pages to your teacher, but lots of things need to happen before that. Brainstorm a list of the steps you need to take and put them in order. Write them down in a notebook to help you remember the different parts and keep track of what you need to do next. Cross off accomplishments as you achieve them, and watch your list get smaller—nothing motivates like progress!

ESSENTIAL SKILLS: LEARNING FROM MISTAKES

Sometimes along the way to accomplishing your goals, you hit a bump in the road. You studied hard but still didn't get the test grade you were shooting for, or you didn't read the directions closely for your assignment and read the wrong section of a book. Believe it or not, slip-ups are part of the learning process. When you don't do things exactly right the first time, it's an opportunity to retrain your brain to think a little differently. It's normal to fumble a few times before getting it right. Rather than spending time beating yourself up about it, use the situation to think about what you can do differently the next time.

Have a Plan B

While coming up with a plan is crucial to success, sometimes even the best plans need a Plan B. As you think about the steps on the way to achieving your goals, ask yourself, "Is there anything that could get in the way of me accomplishing this?" If the answer is yes or maybe, take some time to come up with an alternate plan—just in case.

Chart Your Progress

Sometimes it's hard to see how far you've come until you put it down on paper. Consider having a notebook or an electronic document where you can record the progress you're making. If you're working on improving your test grades, record each test score so that you can see how you're doing. This will also help you focus on your own progress instead of comparing yourself to someone else.

Reward Yourself

Sometimes the satisfaction of getting something done is all the reward we need. But let's be honest—who wouldn't want to have a treat along with that mental satisfaction? Take time to celebrate your hard work and perseverance. Pick out something awesome ahead of time that you will get to do or buy once you've reached your goal. If it's an activity with your friends, put their picture up where you can see it. If it's something you want to buy yourself, put the money in an envelope and label it with the name of the completed goal.

Use this worksheet to focus in on concrete goals and start making progress!

STEP 1:

Pick something that you want to achieve in the next week or month that relates to school.

Write it down here:

_____

_____

_____

STEP 2:

Check to make sure you have set up a SMART goal.

Is your goal:

Specific? Clearly define what you want to achieve

Measurable? Numbers, please

Achievable? Make it doable (even if you have to stretch a little bit)

Relevant? Relate it to the other things that matter most to you

Time-based? Pick a time to start and complete it

Rewrite your goal (if it needs to be SMARTer):

_____

_____

_____

STEP 3:

Set up a plan to make it happen. Remember to break it down to who, what, when, where, and how.

Who: _____

What: _____

When: _____

Where: _____

How: _____

STEP 4:

What else can you do to stay on track?

- ❑ Write it down
- ❑ Tell a friend
- ❑ Picture it
- ❑ Break it down into smaller pieces
- ❑ Come up with a Plan B
- ❑ Chart your progress
- ❑ Set a reward

Chapter 2
Keeping Your Time in Check

Once the school day's over and done with, most students are left facing a whole new set of responsibilities: There's homework to do, music and sports to practice, chores to complete—the list goes on and on. Given that there are only so many hours in a day, you might end up sacrificing your sleep or your downtime in order to stay on track with homework, and who wants that?

By getting a clearer sense of where your time goes and what matters to you most, you can make important decisions that will help you get the most out of your day and avoid unnecessary stress.

Where Does the Time Go?

You probably have a full schedule already, and it probably also changes every day. In order to make the most of the time you *do* have, take stock of your weekly commitments and responsibilities so that you can see how much time, if any, is left over. Then you'll be able to see how much time you really have left for homework, friends, fun, and "you time." Ideally, you want an extra hour each night that isn't already spoken for, so that you have some wiggle room in your schedule for breaks or last-minute studying. And if you're already too booked to complete all of your activities, it's time to consider taking something off your plate.

Your Current Schedule

Create a weekly calendar with all of your current commitments using the worksheet—or an e-calendar, or just a blank piece of paper—to block out the times that are already booked because of

Blank Example Chart

Time	Monday	Tuesday	Wednesday	Thursday	Friday	Saturday	Sunday
6:00 A.M.							
6:30 A.M.							
7:00 A.M							
7:30 A.M.							
8:00 A.M.							
8:30 A.M.							
9:00 A.M.							
9:30 A.M							
10:00 A.M							
10:30 A.M.							
11:00 A.M							
11:30 A.M							
12:00 P.M.							
12:30 P.M							
1:00 P.M							
1:30 P.M							
2:00 P.M.							
2:30 P.M.							
3:00 P.M.							
3:30 P.M.							
4:00 P.M							
4:30 P.M.							
5:00 P.M							
5:30 P.M							
6:00 P.M							
6:30 P.M							
7:00 P.M							
7:30 P.M							
8:00 P.M							
8:30 P.M							
9:00 P.M							
11:00 P.M. to 6:00 A.M. Sleep							

school, travel time, meals, work, or other extracurricular activities. Shade and label the blocks of time with each of your current commitments. Include the time you wake up and travel to and from school, and the time spent doing anything but homework. Leave blocks when you don't have something specifically scheduled open.

Once you've blocked out your "busy time," take stock of the time that's left over, and ask yourself the following questions:

Do I have enough time devoted to my homework?
❏ Yes ❏ No

If you don't know how much time you need, quickly add up how many different assignments you have on an average night and how much time each one takes. It doesn't need to be exact—just estimate how much time you think you'll need. Always budget an extra thirty minutes just in case.

Am I doing my homework during my "prime time"?
❏ Yes ❏ No

Are you a morning person or a night owl? Some people do their best work first thing in the morning, while for other people there's no time like the nighttime. Try and figure out your "prime time" so that you can do your most critical work when your brain works best. Similarly, do your easiest assignments during the times when your energy or motivation is low. And remember that your brain needs rest! So if you're a night owl, make sure you don't have to get up at six in the morning for school. And if you're planning on doing your work in the morning, hit the sheets early.

Do I have enough time to recharge (sleep, hang with friends, watch some TV, etc.)?

❏ Yes   ❏ No

Maybe after a long day of school you need a little downtime before you gear up for homework. Block in some time to unwind, and don't forget that sleep is your friend! Make sure your homework schedule doesn't completely take over your sleep schedule.

Am I scheduling in mini-breaks as I do my homework?

❏ Yes   ❏ No

Studies show that the brain can only take so much before it needs a rest, so be sure to schedule short breaks. The recommended break time is 10 to 15 minutes every hour. (Set an alarm if you need to remind yourself!) During your break, do something to recharge your batteries. Take a walk around the block, comment on some Facebook posts, call a friend, or grab a snack. Whatever you choose, make sure it's something you enjoy . . . but not too much! You want to be able to get back to work when the time is up!

If you answered yes to all of these questions, then skip to "Making the Most Out of Your Time." If you answered no to any of these questions, read on. It's time to assess what you're doing now, and start to make some changes.

Doing What Matters Most

Even though you may want to do it all, sometimes that's just not realistic. Sometimes you'll have to choose what *not* to do.

That choice can often be more difficult than the decision to take something up, because once you've set your mind to something it's hard to let it drop, especially if you really enjoy it or you've already dedicated lots of time to it.

But when things start to slip—when you're not getting enough sleep, when you're getting into arguments with your parents, when your grades start to drop, when you don't have enough time for your friends or yourself—then it's time to make adjustments. And that's okay!

SET YOURSELF UP FOR SUCCESS FROM THE START

Given how competitive the college admissions process is, it's tempting to start doing tons of things that will look good on your transcript or résumé. While this is generally a good idea, you have to be careful or you might end up taking too many AP classes on top of several extracurricular activities, or signing up for an additional club or team that you don't really have time for. Just because you think colleges want to see it, doesn't mean you ought to do it. When signing up for extra classes or activities, go with your gut and do things that connect to what you want for yourself. That way you won't get overwhelmed.

Prioritizing Your Commitments

Here's a quick way to figure out how to determine what matters most to you so that you can make adjustments to your schedule. Start by jotting down all the things you are committed to outside of school. Then, organize the list into "must keep," "willing to give up for now," and "would like to keep."

"Must keep" O

Circle the one *thing* you cannot imagine giving up. This is your "must keep"—your top personal priority, the thing that you just can't give up, either because you love it too much, or because it's non-negotiable (like a job that's critical for you and your family). If you are having trouble coming to a decision, think about the goals you've set for yourself and how each of the things on your list connect to those goals.

"Willing to give up for now (or forever!)" ✓

Put a check mark next to any commitment that it's possible for you to take a brief break from without suffering any major repercussions. These are things that you can easily return to later on, or things that don't matter as much to you. You might even find that you never pick them up again! Either way, it helps you prioritize.

"Would like to keep" 1 *through* 10

Take a look at everything left on the list, and identify how important each one is to you by putting a ranking number beside it. This is your "would like to keep" group—those things that do still matter to you and that you'd like to manage to fit into your schedule.

Adjust Your Weekly Schedule

Now comes the hard part! Once you've organized your list, select one or two additional commitments that you are willing to give up for now. While it might be difficult, you'll breathe easier with the extra time to really focus on the things that matter most to you.

Now that you've made some choices, adjust your schedule using the following guidelines:

1. Make sure you have time blocked out for homework during your prime time.

2. Schedule breaks every 45 minutes or so to recharge your brain and to get a snack, if needed.

3. Schedule some time for yourself, whether it be time with your friends or listening to music.

Case Study: Abby's Schedule

Abby was a high school sophomore with a full plate of extracurricular activities, challenging classes, and a couple of BFFs who always wanted to hang out. However, with such a packed schedule her grades started slipping (especially in physics), and she was struggling in subjects that used to be no problem. She was getting into more arguments with her parents and not getting enough sleep. To try and get a handle on things, she took a look at her weekly schedule to see how she could adjust her priorities.

Schedule: Before Prioritizing

In laying out her schedule, Abby noticed a few things that made her realize she needed to make some changes:

1. She didn't have enough time every day for homework. One and a half hour some nights wasn't cutting it.

2. The time she had slotted for her homework started as late as 9:30 pm, when her brain was already tired—not her prime time for thinking and problem solving.

3. She didn't have any time during the week to relax. No wonder she was so stressed!

Abby's Schedule Before Prioritizing

Time	Monday	Tuesday	Wednesday	Thursday	Friday	Saturday	Sunday
6:00 A.M.	Wake up	Wake up	Wake up	Wake up	Wake up	Sleep	Sleep
6:30 A.M.	6:50 pick up	6:50 pick up	6:50 pick up	6:50 pick up	6:50 pick up		
7:00 A.M		In school		In school			
7:30 A.M.							
8:00 A.M.							
8:30 A.M.							
9:00 A.M.	In school		In school		In school	Long run	
9:30 A.M							
10:00 A.M.							
10:30 A.M.							
11:00 A.M.							
11:30 A.M.							
12:00 P.M.							
12:30 P.M.						Pancakes	
1:00 P.M.							
1:30 P.M.						Karate	
2:00 P.M.							Homework
2:30 P.M.							
3:00 P.M.	Track	Track	Track	Track	Track		
3:30 P.M.							
4:00 P.M							
4:30 P.M							
5:00 P.M.	Snack	Snack		Snack	Snack		
5:30 P.M.							
6:00 P.M.		Community Service	Track or Community Service				
6:30 P.M.	Karate						
7:00 P.M.				Karate			
7:30 P.M.							
8:00 P.M							Homework
8:30 P.M.			Dinner	Homework			
9:00 P.M	Dinner	Dinner	Homework				
9:30 P.M	Homework	Homework					
10:00 P.M							
10:30 P.M.							

11:00 P.M. to 6:00 A.M. Sleep

Schedule: After Prioritizing

Abby made a list of her "must keep," "would like to keep," and "willing to give up" commitments, and made some decisions about how to adjust them. She decided to cut back on her karate classes while track was in season to free up her schedule on Monday and Thursday evenings. She also cut back on her Tuesday-night community service. These adjustments did wonders! Here's how:

1. She had way more time for homework and was able to schedule in time for physics tutoring three times per week.

2. She could do her homework when she was most alert, right after practice and dinner.

3. She was able to schedule in time to relax and see her friends.

Making the Most of Your Time

Once you have a better sense of when you're busy and when you're not, there are a few things you can do to make the most out of every hour in your day. By tracking your daily responsibilities and planning for what's coming up, you'll keep your stress levels low and your productivity high.

Track Everything in One Place

In order to stay in control of your schedule, you'll want to keep a centralized calendar, on your smart phone or day planner. You'll use this to record everything you need to do, including homework assignments, upcoming tests, projects, extracurricular activities, and appointments. Make sure you keep your planner up-to-date by writing in all assignments and activities for the day,

Abby's Schedule After Prioritizing

Time	Monday	Tuesday	Wednesday	Thursday	Friday	Saturday	Sunday
6:00 A.M.	Wake up	Wake up	Wake up	Wake up	Wake up	Sleep	Sleep
6:30 A.M.	6:50 pick up	6:50 pick up	6:50 pick up	6:50 pick up	6:50 pick up		
7:00 A.M		In school		In school			
7:30 A.M.	Homework		Homework		Homework		
8:00 A.M.							
8:30 A.M.							
9:00 A.M.	In school		In school		In school		
9:30 A.M							
10:00 A.M.							
10:30 A.M.							
11:00 A.M.						Long run	
11:30 A.M.							
12:00 P.M.							
12:30 P.M.							
1:00 P.M.						Pancakes	
1:30 P.M.							
2:00 P.M.							
2:30 P.M.							
3:00 P.M.	Track	Track	Track	Track	Track		
3:30 P.M.						Karate	
4:00 P.M							
4:30 P.M							
5:00 P.M.	Snack	Snack		Snack	Snack		
5:30 P.M.	Chill	Chill		Chill	Physics		
6:00 P.M.	Dinner	Dinner	Community service	Dinner		Time with friends	
6:30 P.M.	Physics	Physics		Physics	Time with friends		
7:00 P.M.							
7:30 P.M.							
8:00 P.M.							Homework
8:30 P.M.	Break	Break	Dinner	Break			
9:00 P.M.	Homework	Homework	Homework	Homework			Break
9:30 P.M.							Homework
10:00 P.M.	Break	Break	Break	Break			
10:30 P.M.	Homework	Homework	Homework	Homework			

11:00 P.M. to 6:00 A.M. Sleep

week, and beyond. Remember, you can't find the time to do stuff if you're not clear on what you have to do!

TIME-SAVER: FINDING POCKETS OF TIME

When you have lots going on during the week or on the weekends, it's crucial to take advantage of every pocket of time. Find the minutes in between your packed schedule to knock out part or all of an assignment. Waiting for the bus? Do a few math problems. Waiting for practice to start? Whip out your vocab flash cards. Extra twenty minutes at lunch? Hit the library to start that history assignment. Even if you don't finish, you'll have gotten a head start so the whole assignment won't ambush you later on.

You'll also use your planner to get a clear sense each week of your schedule and commitments. Pay attention to the days when you have major assignments due, and the afternoons or evenings where you have more commitments. If you have commitments that happen every week—say a music lesson on Tuesdays at 6:00 pm—set up a recurring event on your calendar app. If you're using a paper planner, write that event on a Post-it and move it from week to week.

Homework Planning in Two Easy Steps

As tempting as it may be to dive right into your assignments when you get home from school (or not!), the secret to getting it all done is daily planning. No matter how stressed out you are, you should always spend five to ten minutes a day setting up your homework strategy. Planning out your to-do list will actually create more free time, improve your grades, and reduce your stress. So take out your planner (or open your app, as the case may be) and follow this two-step process.

Step 1: Make a List

School assignments generally break down into three core groups: (1) things that are due tomorrow; (2) things that are due by the end of the week; and (3) things that are due at the end of the semester or year. As a result, your own schedule should follow a similar pattern and list assignments according to when they're due—"today," "this week," or "later on." Include all homework assignments (whether they're due the next day or the next week) along with any other commitments you might have, like "pick up my sister" or "bake cookies for fundraiser." Writing it all down clears it out of your mind so you don't have to stress out trying to remember everything. Cross out or check off tasks as you complete them, and as you move through the week shift tasks from "do later" or "do this week" to "do today."

TIME-SAVER: ADDING PADDING

Successful students often have a good sense of how long things will actually take. If you don't leave yourself enough time for tasks, you can end up doing some serious scrambling! If this sounds like you, try this: Write down how much time you think each task will take. Then, set a timer on your phone or computer and actually time yourself. Did you come close? If you tend to underestimate the time that things will take, then it's probably a good idea to include some padding in your schedule. The more time you give yourself, the less stressed you'll be!

Step 2: Prioritize and Organize

With your "today" list in hand, take a minute to think about the order in which you'll do things—and don't just revert to the order of your classes, or whatever happens to be at the top of your list. Instead, you'll want to sort your homework assignments so that you can maximize your time and minimize your stress. In terms of overall efficiency, it makes the most sense to attack the quick and easy stuff before you move on to the important and challenging assignments.

So if there's anything on your list that takes three minutes or less, do that first! For everything else, ask yourself, "How important is this?" If it's critical to the class as a whole, or if it's going to be a major part of your grade, then that should be a top priority item. If it's something that has less of an impact on your overall performance or grade, then you can push to the back of the metaphorical line—for now, that is.

When it comes to homework, the ideal end result is for a student to learn what he needs to learn and do the work he needs to do—but sometimes that just isn't possible. If you're forced to choose from time to time between learning and doing, it's best to try and rely on common sense. But if you feel like you're constantly forced to make that choice, it may be time to get in touch with your teachers, and see if there's something else you could be doing differently.

Planning for Tests and Major Projects

Planning your schedule can get extra tricky when you factor in a big test or a major project. How do you fit those extra big assignments into a schedule that's already packed? The secret is to break the big projects down into smaller chunks, so that your schedule remains balanced and spread out. It's always easier to deal with a lot of small pieces rather than one giant chunk. With that noble goal in mind, we now offer the secret to successful test and project planning, in three easy steps…

THREE PROCRASTINATION BUSTERS

Stop thinking. Start doing. We waste a lot of time thinking about what we should be doing rather than doing it.

Do the easiest thing first. You'll feel a great sense of accomplishment when you start to see immediate progress.

Do something difficult. Often whatever we are avoiding is much worse in our minds than it is in reality. So get out there and bring the fight to the project! You'll feel really empowered when you clear the first major hurdle.

Step 1: Set Your Own Deadlines

Pull out your calendar—or your calendar app—and write down when the big assignment or test is due. Then break down the steps that need to get completed by that day. (Sometimes your teacher does this for you by requiring you to turn in parts of the assignment along the way. If so, write down those deadlines on your calendar.) What concepts do you need to know for that test? What topics will you need to cover in that presentation? Whatever it is that you need to get done, write it down!

Step 2: Break It Down Even More

Once you've got the deadlines set, break things down even more. If you need to turn in 100 note cards in two weeks, break it down to 20 cards over five different nights. If you need to learn all the bones in the hand, try and memorize one finger at a time. This makes those big and intimidating tasks seem much more manageable . . . and much less annoying.

Step 3: Put the Steps on Your Calendar

Take those smaller tasks and put them on your calendar. As you create your daily plan, be sure to include them on your list. Tempted to blow them off because the deadline is way out there? Bad idea! That distant deadline will be here faster than you think. Keep track of everything on your calendar, though, and you won't be caught off guard.

One last thing

Do yourself a favor: Don't procrastinate! It's so easy to leave the big assignments until the last minute. But the bigger they are, the more time you'll need. That's why major projects are assigned in advance. The longer you wait, the more stressed out you'll get. It's just not worth it!

Keep Your Parents on Your Side *and* off Your Back

If you're like most other teens, you are going to have a few blowups with your parents about school. Whether it's about how much time you are, or are not, spending on your work or what grades you're earning, chances are there are going to be a few times a month when you feel like your parents are too much in your business.

Remember, the reason that they ask is because they care. As you take more responsibility for your work, your parents don't necessarily see everything you do and therefore wonder what's getting done. They probably aren't really interested in what geometry proofs you are working on that night, but rather want to know that you are doing them (and all your other homework, for that matter). To find out, parents might nag you or start interrogating you. Things can get really uncomfortable and annoying.

How can you change those interactions to make them positive rather than positively awful? To get your parents on your side and off your back, keep them informed about what's going on *before* they have to ask.

Keep Them in the Loop

The main reason that parents have a reputation for badgering kids about school is that most kids don't offer up much information. And that makes sense. On the one hand, it's perfectly reasonable to want to just lock yourself in your room after a long day at school; but by being just a little bit more forthcoming about the projects you're working on, the tests you've taken, and the homework you've been assigned, you'll reduce your parents' anxiety and nip interrogations in the bud. If your parents think you're hiding information, they'll be more inclined to keep pushing even after you've answered the usual questions. But if they trust that you know what you have to do and are capable of getting it done on your own (that is, without parental oversight), then they'll be that much more likely to provide you with the space you need to do your work your way. Everybody wins!

WHAT IS YOUR MINDSET?

In her book *Mindset: The New Psychology of Success*, Carol Dweck describes how the way you *think* about your abilities has a big impact on your ability to try something new or difficult. Some people have a "fixed mindset" (i.e., "I'm only so smart or talented"), while others have a "growth mindset" (i.e., "If I work hard I can do better"). It's not hard to figure out which outlook lends itself more readily to new challenges!

Chapter 3
Getting Your Head in the Game

Ever find that you can memorize every stat of your favorite NFL player or the lyrics to your favorite song but can't for the life of you keep track of those geometry proofs? Learning is much easier if the subject is something you are interested in. When you find yourself gravitating to anything and everything about a topic—books, discussions, podcasts, TV shows, or blogs—you're on your way to becoming an expert! Whether you're reading, writing, talking about it, or actually doing it, the more you immerse yourself in something, the better you'll understand it.

The problem is, school is school. Not everything will grab your attention in the same way, and attention is what primes your brain for learning. So how do you make yourself interested in something that you didn't really care about before? Let's be straight here: It's hard. But it's not impossible! Here are a few strategies you can use to help make it easier.

Adjust Your Attitude

One way to get your head in the game is to adjust your attitude. Only you can decide if you are going to like or want to do something. Only you have the power to define your experience. How, you ask? There are two easy ways to change the way you think about your abilities or interact with a particular subject: 1) Rewrite the story, and 2) embrace challenges.

HOW DO I BENEFIT FROM CHALLENGES?

Think about a time that you were really challenged by something and you found a way to figure it out. Maybe it was learning to hit a fast-ball or doing a tricky math problem. How awesome did you feel after you finally succeeded? Would you have felt as proud if you hadn't kept working at it? Trust me: Challenges *can* be good for you.

Rewrite the Story

Ever feel like you're not so great at something? Whether it's because you didn't get good grades in a particular class, or because you find a subject super-boring or super-difficult, it's normal to start to really dislike something if you don't feel very good at it. That outlook becomes the story you tell yourself over and over again: "I'm just not good at_____," is a pretty definitive story, and—what's worse—it breeds a kind of defeatism.

So why not rewrite the story? Instead of saying "I'm not good at x;" "I'm not good at x *yet.*" Remember, you have the power to define your experience, so why not change the ending of that story? Think positive—and change your story regarding a subject or task that you don't really like.

Rather than going negative, try going positive. Think about a subject you don't like or a skill you don't have, and plug it into your current story.

Now, whenever you get discouraged, tell yourself the new story. And keep saying it over and over again. Soon you will notice your attitude change and you will be more optimistic about the hard stuff.

Embrace Challenges

According to psychologist Carol Dweck, people think about challenges in two different ways. Either you embrace them because they lead to learning and growth, or you avoid them because they are hard and you don't want to fail. Her research shows that the most successful people are those with the growth mindset—those people who embrace challenges! Think again about Michael Jordan: He got cut sophomore year from the varsity basketball team. Did he quit basketball? No, he embraced the challenge and worked even harder to make the varsity team the next year.

We often tell ourselves not-so-great stories about our own abilities, especially if a task has been challenging. That can be a total motivation-killer. If you flip that story around and look at the challenges as opportunities, you'll find yourself succeeding at things you never thought you'd be able to do. Now *that's* a good story.

Get Involved in What You're Learning

It's tempting to tear through an assignment to check it off your list, but you probably won't remember much the next week or even the next day. And since you know it'll probably show up again soon (and—ugh!—probably on a test) it's worthwhile to make sure it sticks the first time. You want to set yourself up for learning, rather than just completing assignments .

There's a big difference between just getting your homework done and actually learning the material. Getting it done means the info is on the page. Learning it means that it's also—at least partially—in your head.

Some assignments don't involve much mental muscle (coloring in a map for your geography class), while others do (creating a lab report for chemistry). Successful students know the difference between high-value and low-value assignments and put in effort accordingly.

For the high-value assignments—those that are worth lots of points or include stuff that's going to be on the test—getting involved with what you are learning will help get it not only onto the paper but into your head.

Getting the Most out of Your Homework

Before you dive into your assignment, you should know why it's important. Think about the specific reason for doing the work, and how it will be applied in your class. Then, ask yourself what you need to do for each assignment. Do you need to memorize information, develop really fantastic study notes, or apply a concept in an essay? Spend your time on that assignment doing those things so you can maximize your efforts.

Record Your Questions and Comments as You Go

Write down any questions or ideas that come to mind as you work through your assignment. If you don't quite understand something or don't know how one idea connects to another, record those thoughts. You might ask anything from, "Why did women support the temperance movement?" to, "What's the difference between mitosis and meiosis?" If the answers are not clear by the time you are finished with the assignment, ask your teacher or a friend in class. By the time you're finished, you'll understand the material much better.

Make Connections

Find ways to link the stuff you're learning to the stuff you already know to help you learn new information faster. Making these connections helps move things into your long-term memory. To do this, think about the ways that what you are learning is similar to or different from what you already know. For example, you can ask yourself, "How is this ecosystem proof similar to another one I learned?"

Doing this accomplishes two things: First, it helps make you curious, which opens your mind to new things and makes you a better learner. Second, connecting what you're learning to what you already know makes things easier to remember. Which, in the long run, will help you to be more successful in and out of school.

Don't Let Obstacles Get in Your Way

It's easy to get frustrated and give up when you try something and it doesn't work. Whether it's a physics problem set, a broken printer, or a group member who isn't pulling their weight, it's easy to get discouraged when you run into roadblocks. One of the keys to success, according to Carol Dweck, is to find ways to work around these roadblocks rather than give up. So when things aren't going your way, here are a few things to try:

Ask for help

Determine your options for additional help. Does your school or teacher offer after-school tutoring? Can a parent, relative, or friend help you? Can you find study guides on the internet?

Take a break

Sometimes we get stuck because we are tired, or we've become bleary-eyed from staring at the same three paragraphs for 40 minutes. When exhaustion creeps in, take a five- to 15-minute break and clear your head. Walk around the house, get a snack, or listen to your favorite song. Solutions often become clear when you walk away for a little while, and then come back with fresh eyes.

Don't give up

Sometimes solutions don't come right away. Try different approaches. Start over. Sometimes you will miss something the first time that is obvious when you do it again.

$\log_a x = \dfrac{\log b}{\log b a}$

y's
$e t$

$\dfrac{(x')^2}{(\sqrt{2})^2} - \dfrac{(y')^2}{(\sqrt{2})^2} = 1$

HERON'S AREA

$\text{Area} = \sqrt{s(s-a)(s-b)(s-c)}$

where $s = (a+b+c)/2$

$\cot 2\theta = \dfrac{A-C}{B}$

$B \neq 0$

formula

$\dfrac{\pi}{2}$

Receiver

3'

O

5

$= 5 \cos 3\theta$

$\theta' = 72°$

$-72°$

θ'

$2\cos^2 x - 3\cos x + 1 = 0$

$(2\cos x - 1)(\cos x - 1) = 0$

a

$e = \dfrac{c}{a} \quad \dfrac{\text{(focus)}}{\text{(distance)}}$

ECCENTRICITY

$b = 27.4 ft$ $102.3°$ a

$28.7°$

A c

$6 \dfrac{2}{2} z$

2

1

$\dfrac{\pi}{2}$ π $\dfrac{3\pi}{2}$ 2π

$os A)7$

PART 2

Staying Classy

Most students spend the majority of their day in school, so unless you're nocturnal, you need to make that time count for something! Figuring out how to take advantage of your time in class is of course essential, but so is learning how to work well with all your teachers. (After all, they're the ones who give out the grades!)

The overall goal here is improved academic performance, but there comes a point where, in addition to learning how to help yourself, you need to figure out how to let others help you as well. That's where Part 2 comes in. The chapters in this section of the book are intended to help you get along better with your teachers, participate more in class, stay on top of your work, and stand up for yourself when you need to.

Chapter 4
Grades and Expectations

Each class you take in high school is like a different country. Each has its own leader, rules, and culture. It's your job to figure out the rules and culture as quickly as possible. In addition, you want to make sure you understand how the country's currency (aka its grading system) works, so that you don't wind up wasting your time on things that aren't really worth anything.

Understand What Your Teacher Expects from You

Your teachers are constantly giving you clues about what it takes tosucceed in their classes. Successful students tend to figure this out in the first few weeks by listening carefully to the class rules and expectations and paying attention to the comments they receive back on their first few assignments.

As you have probably come to appreciate, each teacher has a slightly different way of doing things and different expectations. Some might not care if you turn your assignment in late, while others don't accept any late work, *ever.* As you begin a class, be sure to understand each teacher's expectations as well as your options for getting extra help or turning in late work.

Learn the Rules

Do you know your teacher's classroom rules? Can you chew gum, eat, or drink water in class? Is it okay to record your homework on your cell phone? What's the late-work policy? Knowing the answers to these questions will cut out a lot of the guesswork and make your job as a student that much easier.

On the first day of class, your teachers will usually give you a handout detailing the classroom policies, participation requirements, and grading guidelines. Pay close attention, and if your teacher doesn't go over everything in class, be sure to read the whole handout carefully on your own. Look for important information, like policies for late work, make-up work, and grading, as well as opportunities to come in for extra help. If something is unclear, don't be shy about asking.

THE FIRST-WEEK SHUFFLE

As the new school year begins there are often scheduling conflicts that have to get resolved, with a lot of chaos usually resulting. If you suddenly find yourself in a new class, ask the teacher what papers you missed, what assignments you need to make up and when, and what special supplies you need for class. The fact that you weren't there from the beginning generally doesn't hold much water as an excuse, so be proactive, and do what you can to make up for lost time.

Know Your Options

Even the very best students sometimes need to turn something in late or stay after school for extra help. What if you couldn't figure out how to do the last section of math problems, or you came down with the flu over the weekend? Can you turn in late work? How many points will you lose, if any? When is your teacher available for extra help? Armed with this information, you can set yourself up for success and avoid doing extra, unnecessary work.

Learn the Grading System

Not all points are created equal. Each teacher has her own grading system and decides how each of your assignments will be valued. By understanding your teacher's system, you can figure out which assignments you need to really nail and which ones don't count as much toward your grade. You can then spend your time and extra effort on the stuff that matters most. And now that many teachers are posting grades online, you can check in and see how things are going on a regular basis.

There are two main ways that teachers calculate grades. Some use total points and others use a weighted categories system.

Total Points

"Total points" means that every grade you get goes into a pool of points. At the end of the semester your grade is calculated according to a straight percentage of points earned over points possible. Teachers will designate different point values to an assignment based on how important it is. For example, quizzes might be worth 10 points, while tests are 100 points. Your final grade is a percentage of total points earned over total points possible.

Weighted Categories

Each category is assigned a particular value, or weight. This means that some categories affect your grade more than others. For example, in your science class, tests could be worth 50%, while quizzes might be worth 20%, homework 20%, and participation 10%. For those of you who love taking tests, this is great news. If you're not one of those people, you might want to work on your test-taking skills. Let's see how the weighted system might look for two students whose averages are the same for all their work except for tests. Notice how Student B's overall grade is much lower due to his lower grades on tests:

Category	Weight	Student A	Student B
Tests	50%	95%	77%
Quizes	20%	87%	87%
Homework	20%	93%	93%
Participation	10%	92%	92%
Total		**92.7%**	**83.7%**

How do you calculate your grade by yourself using the weighted system? Using the example from Student A: tests 95% weighted at 50% (95 x .5 = 47.5 points), quizzes 87% weighted at 20% (87 x .2 = 17.4 points), etc. Add them all together to get your total points out of 100 (92.7/100) and your final grade percentage (92.7%). Phew!

Knowing the value of assignments helps you decide what you should spend most of your time on. If you have to choose between studying for a test and finishing a homework assignment, you can prioritize your time by checking how much each assignment affects your final grade.

Take Responsibility for Your Education

The further you progress in your education, the more teachers and parents will expect you to manage your own workload and assignments. One of the biggest shocks to students when they start high school is how much less attentive teachers are to the submissions of individual assignments. Instead, it's up to you to track your work.

Why should you have to take the responsibility? For one thing, you have way fewer teachers (six or seven) than your teachers have students (100–150). It can be challenging for them to remember who needs what and when. So whether you don't understand something or you've fallen behind and need help getting back on track, work with your teacher to make a plan that works for both of you.

Track Your Assignments

The most successful students develop a way to record, plan, and track their assignments. This helps you manage your time (see Chapter 2) and make sure that your work is done correctly. Whether you use a good old-fashioned printed school calendar, an online calendar, or a smartphone app, be sure to consistently record the details.

Keep Your Teacher in the Loop!

There will be times when you have to miss school, or you need some extra help with a tough assignment. Whether you miss class because you are sick, or need to leave early for a sports event, it's up to you to get in touch with your teacher as soon as you can.

Let your teacher know in advance that you are missing school and find out how she would like you to make up the class work or assignments. Find a good time to talk, like before or after school, or during a free period. If you aim for a long conversation five minutes before class starts, you probably won't get very far. If all else fails, e-mail your teacher to find out when you can meet or what assignments you can start on.

Know Your Resources

Another strategy for success is to know your resources. There are guaranteed to be times when you'll need help—everyone does!— and you'll need to know where you can turn. If your teacher has a blog or website, bookmark it. If you have a tendency to forget your homework (or lose your notes), write down the contact information for at least two people from each of your classes (e-mail and phone number). Finally, know the internet resources available through your school library. Many schools give you access to online databases that make researching much easier than just using a search engine.

If you need extra help learning a concept, working through a problem set, or writing a paper, you can also seek additional help outside of class from teachers and tutors.

Tutors

Some schools provide free after-school tutoring programs. The tutors might be teachers from the school, community volunteers, or upperclassmen. This is a great opportunity to get one-on-one help and can give you a real boost. Do a little research to find out what your school offers.

Teachers

Many teachers are happy to work with students one-on-one before school, during lunch, or after school. Some teachers have set times that they're available and when you can just drop in, while others prefer their students to make definite appointments. Spending a little extra time with your teacher will not only help you do better in the class but will also show your teacher that you are committed to, and taking responsibility for, your education.

Navigating Different Teaching Styles

Your teacher sets the stage for your experience in everything that happens in class. She decides what matters most, evaluates the quality of your work, and sets the tone for the class experience as a whole. There will be some teachers that you love, some that you tolerate, and some that you can't stand—and that's perfectly natural—but when times get tough it's worth remembering that your teacher got into this business for a reason: because she wanted to help kids to learn! And even though it may seem like teachers' rules exist just to ruin your life, that's probably not their primary purpose.

Teachers come in many different varieties, but there are some core personas that teachers tend to adopt as a means of communicating their values and priorities to students. As a student it's worth familiarizing yourself with these personas so that you can be the student your teacher wants you to be (if only for that one class). And who knows, you may even become more virtuous in the process!

One other thing worth mentioning before we get down to details: Working with lots of different types of people—whether they're teachers or classmates or administrators—is something you'll be doing for your entire life. So you might as well start getting good at it now!

The way you act in class and the effort you make will have a great influence on how smoothly things go for you. But no matter how much effort you put in, and how charming you may actually be, no one goes through school without a few conflicts of personality. So let's look at a few common teaching styles that tend to give students problems, and see how you can deal with them.

TEACHERS AS MENTORS

If you have a teacher that you really get along with, do your best to stay in touch with her even after you're done with her class. It's great to have mentors in your life: They can offer advice and guidance as you encounter challenging new life decisions, and they can help with letters of recommendation in a pinch! Teachers got into the business because they like working with young people, so take advantage of that inclination, and see what your teachers can do for you!

The Stickler

The Stickler is the teacher who just wants his students to follow the rules. He usually has very definite ideas about classroom behavior and protocol, and wants students to listen to instructions, follow instructions, and not waste his or his classroom's time on the little stuff. Stickler-types often enforce order on the classroom by penalizing students for not writing their names at the top right corner, for instance, or packing up their backpacks before class is over. If you don't naturally conduct your life in an organized fashion, the Stickler can present some real problems, and lead to unnecessarily discounted scores and grades.

What the Stickler hates: More than anything else he hates it when instructions are repeatedly ignored—or appear to be ignored.

Why the Stickler has a point: Whether we're doing our taxes or getting a passport or just crossing the street, rules set the boundaries of our existence and enable us to get things done in a more efficient fashion. We all have bad habits that we could stand to lose, and even though the specific rules that your teacher enforces may not have much application after the school day is over, it's still a good exercise to try and teach yourself to behave a little differently. The Stickler presents students with an opportunity to grow!

How to respond: Do your best to learn the rules and follow them. If you do have a tendency to make a certain mistake, let your teacher know that you recognize the problem and are making an effort to remedy it. Then, even if you continue to make that error on occasion, your teacher will know that you aren't doing it out of a lack of a respect for the class or its system.

The Idealist

The Idealist generally presides over a more chaotic kind of environment, where rules are less important than learning, students take the initiative in discussions, and enthusiasm has a real role in the classroom. Idealists want students who want to learn. This can, however, lead to problems if you're the kind of student who has trouble keeping organized, or who needs a lot of oversight.

What the Idealist hates: Apathy. You've got to show the Idealists of the world that you care about your own education.

Why the Idealist has a point: School is hard, and learning takes effort. Students aren't going to get very far if they can't find a way of getting invested in and excited about the material!

How to respond: This is the kind of classroom where class performance really matters. Do your best to demonstrate your willingness to try. For the most part, Idealistic teachers are willing to put extra effort in where students have put extra effort in on their own already. So be the kind of student they can root for!

The Realist

The Realist is the teacher who acknowledges the limits of what she can do on her own. She's clear about the assignments, straightforward about her expectations, and relatively unforgiving of faults in students (a Realist, by definition, isn't interested in fantastical homework excuses).

What the Realist hates: When students waste her time.

Why the Realist has a point: Teaching is not an easy job. It's time and labor intensive, and in many cases the students that teachers are responsible for are openly hostile to their mission.
In terms of emotional efficiency, it just makes sense to invest the time where it's going to have a real effect.

How to respond: If you treat your teacher with respect and do the assignments seriously, you won't have any problems with the Realists of the world. Treat the Realist's classroom as you would a place of work, and avoid making grand gestures or being openly dismissive. Don't waste her time, and she won't waste yours.

The Intellectual

The Intellectual is the kind teacher who engages in dialogue with his students. The classroom, in his hands, becomes a kind of experiment in learning. In good times, this encourages student involvement and really motivates a classroom, but at the worst of times this can slow down progress and leave students scrambling for the information that really matters.

What the Intellectual hates: Passivity. Conversations can't happen in a room full of listeners. There needs to be some talking too!

Why the Intellectual has a point: Like the Idealist, the Intellectual is looking for ways to make the students really care about the material.

How to respond: Help yourself and help the class by asking questions that engage with the key points directly—and if you're not sure what the key points are, then ask!

The Motivational Speaker

The Motivational Speaker has a bright outlook on almost everything—except defeatism. She's available to prop you up when you're feeling discouraged, and even if your recent performances have resembled a sinking ship more than a bird in flight, she's willing to work with you to find a solution or a way to improve your performance. The encouragement can really be a boon to a struggling student, but the positive outlook can also mask a student's underperformance if they wind up focusing more on the style of the teacher's address than on the substance of what she's saying.

What the Motivational Speaker hates: When students aren't pro-active.

Why the Motivational Speaker has a point : It's lazy to give up. A little bit of effort tends to go a long way, and the more you put in, the more you get out. These ideas are trite, sure, but they continue to circulate because they have a lot of truth to them!

How to respond: Make an honest effort! Try and improve! If your teacher can see you working at it, she'll also make herself available to find solutions when you run out of answers yourself. (And if you ever need a confidence boost, be sure to pay her a visit!)

One last word on teachers and teaching styles:

These are rough outlines: No one teacher is just a Stickler, or just a Realist. Instead, teachers make use of these tactics in a way that complements their own personality and adds something to the class. So keep an open mind, listen to what your teacher is telling you, try and accommodate her preferences, and if you ever hit an impasse or don't know quite what to do anymore, go and talk to her.

Chapter 5
Working the Classroom

We've covered how to work best with your teacher, but there are also some tried-and-true strategies for success that will help you interact with almost anyone. And while all these tips are given with the classroom in mind, they should also help you in your life outside of school . . . like when you start looking for—ack!—a job.

Successful students do a few things that help them quickly make their mark in the classroom. They make a good impression, stay on top of their work, participate actively in class, and know how to get and stay focused.

First Impressions

You only get to make a first impression once, so make sure you nail it. At the beginning of each school year, you have an opportunity to show everyone your best self. In some cases, if you have an older brother or sister who had the same teacher, you need to make sure the teacher understands how you are (or— ahem—are not!) like your sibling. Your teacher will base his first impressions on how you conduct yourself early on in class, and on the first assignments you turn in, so show some enthusiasm and knock those assignments out of the park.

Show Enthusiasm

You can make a good impression on your teacher by being engaged in class. This doesn't mean that you have to act like everything your teacher says is amazing. Just pay close attention, sit up in your chair, and look at the person who is speaking. Most teachers pick subjects they are really into, so it will go a long way if you can demonstrate your interest in the class discussion.

Nail Your First Assignments

As mentioned before, many teachers will form impressions of you based on the first few assignments you turn in. So if you turn in your best work right away, your teacher will see you as a good student and a hard worker. Later on, she might give you the benefit of the doubt if you don't quite come through. You also want to show your teacher what you can do, so she can understand your strengths and areas for growth. That way, you'll get the kind of feedback you need in order to do better in class. It's a win-win situation.

WEATHERING THE FIRST FEW WEEKS

Your grade is based on how many total points you earn out of a maximum number. Simple, right? Well, sort of. What's interesting about grades is that early on in the semester, missing one assignment has a *big* impact on your overall grade, because there are fewer total points at the beginning of the year. Don't despair—you can catch up later, but you might see an unwanted progress report along the way. Solution: Always turn something in.

For your first assignments in particular, take care to be extra neat and format the document the way the teacher requests it. Even just turning in a neat paper makes a positive impression.

And turn those assignments in on time! Missing one assignment at the beginning of the year can really hurt your grade and give your teacher the impression that you won't complete your future work on time. There are going to be plenty of times later on in the year that you might need to turn something in late, so you don't want to start off the year making special requests.

Staying On Top of Your Work

As we discussed in Part 1, success in school depends to a large extent upon your ability to manage and parcel out your time. And it's not always easy, I know! In order to stay on top of your work you'll need to make a plan (so that you can actually finish what's assigned), get organized (so that you can find what you need when you need it), and start early (so that you don't wind up overwhelmed at the end). But there's also a lot that you can do while still in class to cut down on unnecessary stress later on...

Write Everything Down

After taking notes in class, make sure to keep everything in a place where it's easy to access and hard to lose. And if your teacher gives you some extra details about how she wants the homework done, write those details down, too! Then use your assignment list to prioritize what needs to be done when and in what order.

You probably have a pretty good memory, but you still might forget one critical detail (or even the whole assignment) by the time you get home. Your brain has plenty to remember—so leave the details to your planner.

TIME-SAVER: APPS AND E-CALENDARS

Interested in going paperless? Depending on your device, you might choose to use an app or an online calendar. Some apps are strictly mobile, while others sync with your computer. Check out iStudiez Pro, iHomework, or myHomework if you want something designed just for school. If you are using an online calendar like iCal or Google Calendar, make sure you record the assignment's due date so that you can keep track of what's coming up rather than when it was assigned.

No matter what paperless method you choose, be sure it's backed up just in case it gets lost, stolen, or broken.

Participation

Multiple studies show that the more ways you engage with your material, the better you learn. In fact, after you discuss something you've heard or read, you're twice as likely to retain that information. That's why teachers award participation grades. Class is way more interesting when people are actually sharing their thoughts, and you just might learn something!

For some people, participation can be terrifying. No one wants to ask a "dumb" question or say something that makes you feel embarrassed. And being called on by the teacher might be intimating, especially if you don't know the answer. To give yourself more confidence, try these tips that make participation less scary and more fun.

Prepare Thoughtfully

As you do your assignment for class, write down any questions or comments you have about the material. If you're taking notes, highlight sections that you found interesting or that you had questions about. This way, if you're called on, you won't get stuck with your mouth hanging open! Take another look at your assignment as class starts so the material is fresh in your mind.

Listen Carefully

Listen to what others say so that you can build on the conversation, instead of just repeating what others have already said. Sometimes we're so busy developing our own future comments that we don't pay attention to what's actually going on in class now. If something pops into your head while someone else is talking, jot it down quickly and then keep listening! When your classmate has stopped speaking, you can then determine whether what you wrote down adds something to the overall dialogue or not; and if it doesn't, then just move on!

Classroom Geography

Sit in a part of the classroom where you can hear and see well. It's easier to tune things out in the back of the class . . . and easier to hide, too. Be brave! Sit up front where the teacher can see you, and let your awesomeness shine.

Allow Others to Speak

Part of being a good participant is letting others make comments. Most teachers' participation guidelines include something about not "dominating" the discussion. If you've just made a comment, hold off—even if you know the answer. If you need help slowing yourself down, try counting from 1 to 10 before you raise your hand again, and this way, you can give your less enthusiasite classmates an opportunity to speak.

LOCATION, LOCATION, LOCATION

If you're able to choose your seat, find a spot that works for you. Often times the place you'd *like* to be—like next to your friends, or in the back of the class—is not the place you ought to be. If you have a hard time paying attention when you're sitting next to friends, it's easy enough to find an excuse to sit somewhere else. (But you still have to make yourself do it.) And if all the cool kids sit in the back of the class, the same rule applies: Just say you want to be near the window, and move further up where there's still room. If you know your weaknesses and resolve to address them, there's always a way to find a solution.

Respect Other Ideas

You don't have to agree with your classmates . . . but you *do* have to respect their ideas. If you're opposed to someone else's argument, take the diplomatic route and say, "I disagree with what you *said* because . . ." Let them know it's what they said and not them that you disagree with. This keeps the conversation focused on the ideas, and doesn't make it a personal attack.

Ask Questions

Sometimes we feel embarrassed when we ask questions. But if you don't understand something, chances are you're not the only one. A huge part of learning is asking questions, so if you're not sure about something, ask! Your classmates will silently thank you later.

Zoning In vs. Zoning Out

You have a tough job as a student. You go from class to class with very few breaks in between. If you're like most other people, there's one part of the day where you inevitably find yourself zoning out. Whether it's during your third class in a row, just after a big lunch, or in the middle of a concept you just can't grasp, staying focused can be hard. So what do you do to keep those lids from sagging?

There are a couple of things you can do to keep yourself in the game. Force yourself to ask questions, especially if you don't understand something. Chances are if you don't get it now, then you'll be even more lost if you wait ten minutes. Also, work on developing a trick to keep your mind sharp. It might be taking notes (even if you don't feel like it), doodling, chewing gum, squeezing a ball, drinking water, or sitting up straight. Figure out what works for you. And, in case you forgot: Get some sleep! (After class is over, of course.)

When to Zone In

You're being introduced to new material every day, and you're learning all the time (at least we hope so!). If you want to do well, here are some key moments during class when you'll really want to pay attention.

During a lecture or discussion

Your teacher will usually make it obvious when she's about to give you some vital information. She'll say things like, "This is important," and "this will be on the test." She might also pause to get the class's attention or repeat something. When this happens, listen up! This is something you need to know, so write it down in your notes to study later. If you don't understand, then make sure to ask questions during class or find time later to get help from your teacher, a friend, or a parent.

Assignment explanations

There's nothing worse than getting home and having no idea what you're supposed to do for your homework. Perhaps you wrote down, "English worksheet," in your planner, but when you pull it out there are no directions. You vaguely remember the teacher saying something about only doing the odd numbers— or was it the evens? You then spend the next 20 minutes Facebooking your friends to figure out what you're supposed to do, when you could have spent that time actually completing the assignment. If your teacher gives you extra directions, write them down! Preferably it's on the worksheet or in your planner, but if the only thing available is your hand, use it!

Major projects often require several steps and a lot of planning. When introducing a big assignment, your teacher might offer a few hints that are sometimes not included on the assignment sheet. This is your opportunity to take some additional notes, ask clarifying questions, and figure out how you're going to tackle this big project. By the time you leave class, you should understand all the different parts of the project so that you can set up your plan of action, with plenty of time to get things done.

Chapter 6
Taking Notes

In most, if not all classes, you will be asked to take notes during a lecture or discussion, or for a reading assignment. Notes help you record the key points and supporting details of what you're learning. Depending on the class, you can use those notes to help you with your homework, review for a test, or write a paper.

The Importance of Good Note-Taking

You might think taking notes is no big deal—how hard can it be to write stuff down, right? But it can actually be challenging to write things down accurately and still pay attention to what your teacher is saying. Becoming a good note-taker takes both practice and finding a system that best suits your style. But if you can learn to take good notes it can help your performance in several very important ways...

It Helps You Manage Your Homework

With so much going on in your life, you're bound to forget a thing or two in the course of the school day. Between first-period math and the time you get home, you've had six or seven classes, gone to drama practice, and maybe stopped at the library, too. There's a good chance that what made perfect sense in class could be a little hazy by now. The same thing goes for the assignments that were passed out. If you weren't clear in your notes, it will be hard to remember which chapters you were supposed to read, and what issues you were supposed to focus on.

It Helps You Stay Focused in Class

By giving yourself a task (taking notes, in this case) you have to focus enough on what's been said to get it down on paper. You should also make sure you sit somewhere that you can see the board clearly and hear what the teacher and your classmates are saying.

It Helps You Actually Learn the Material

Many people learn by writing things down. It's part of the way the brain processes information. By taking what's covered in class and putting it down on paper you begin the learning process right away.

Different Types of Notes

There are several different types of notes you can choose from. In the sections below we cover and give examples of three of the most popular note-taking styles: bulleted notes, outline notes, and Cornell notes. Give each a try and see which one works for you—there's no one best style. If you're taking notes by hand, all three can work; if you're using a computer, play around with the different note-taking formatting options. Feel free to mix and match the parts you like to create a truly effective style.

Bulleted Notes

Bulleted notes use dots and dashes to indicate where a new line of information starts. Indentation is used to show hierarchy— how different bits of information relate to each other in terms of importance. The main topics are furthest to the left, with subtopics and supporting details moving out to the right.

SAMPLE BULLETED NOTES

Aquatic biomes
- Cover 75% of earth's surface
- = Relationship to terrestrial biomes
  - Life depends on oxygen
  - Photosynthesis a source of energy in food chain
- Divided between freshwater & marine
- Most organisms only live in one

Marine
- 35,000 ppm dissolved salts
- 5 zones (proximity to shore)
  - Intertidal zone—land meets water
  - Pelagic – open ocean any depth
  - Benthic – sea floor
  - Photic – w/in 100m of surface = photosynthesis
  - Aphotic – >100m photosynthesis fauna debris

Coral reefs
- Tropical warm H_2O
- Formed by cnidarian
- Grow w/algae
- Sensitive to pollution
- Size/health decreasing

Estuaries
- Fresh H_2O runs to ocean
- Surrounded by marshes
- Drained by humans = bad
- Most productive eco region

Freshwater

SAMPLE OUTLINED NOTES

I. <u>Aquatic biomes</u>

    a. Cover 75% of earth's surface

    b. = Relationship to terrestrial biomes

        i. Life depends on oxygen

        ii. Photosynthesis source of energy in food chain

    c. Divided between freshwater & marine

        i. Most organisms only live in one

II. <u>Marine</u>

    a. 35,000 ppm dissolved salts

    b. 5 zones (proximity to shore)

        i. Intertidal zone – land meets water

        ii. Pelagic – open ocean any depth

        iii. Benthic – sea floor

        iv. Photic – w/in 100m of surface = photosynthesis

        v. Aphotic – >100m photosynthesis fauna debris

    c. Coral reefs

        i. Tropical warm H_2O

        ii. Formed by cnidarian

        iii. Grow w/algaes

        iv. Sensitive to pollution

        v. Size/health decreasing

    d. Estuaries

        i. Fresh H_2O runs to ocean

        ii. Surrounded by marshes

        iii. Drained by humans = bad

        iv. Most productive eco region

III. <u>Freshwater</u>

SAMPLE CORNELL NOTES

Keywords	Notes
Aquatic biomes	Cover 75% of earth's surface—Life depends on oxygen (= terrestrial) 2 kinds ⟶ Marine ⟶ Freshwater Most organisms only live in one
Marine biome	5 zones intertidal zone—land meets water photic—w/in 100m of surface= photosynthesis pelagic—open ocean any depth benthic—sea floor aphotic—> 100m = photosynthesis
Unique environments of Marine biome	Coral reefs ⟶ Tropical warm H20 Formed by cnidarian Grow w/algaes Sensitive to pollution Size/health decreasing Estuaries ⟶ Fresh H20 runs to ocean Surrounded by marshes Drained by humans = bad Most productive eco region

Summary

Aquatic biomes cover 75% of the earth and are made up of the marine and freshwater biomes. The marine biome is made up of 5 different zones that relate to the distance to the shore and ability to use photosynthesis for making food. There are two unique environments in this biome: coral reefs (tropical warm water) and estuaries (fresh water running to the ocean).

Outline Notes

Outline notes use Roman numerals to indicate where a new line of information starts. Indentation is also used to show hierarchy. Many word-proccessing programs make it easy to type using outline notes.

Cornell Notes

Cornell notes (named for the university where they were created by Professor Walter Pauk) use a combination of note-taking and summary to help you condense and organize your notes. Start by dividing the page into two columns, with the left column being about ¼ the width of the page (enough room for key words) and the right column taking the rest of the page. Label the left column "keywords," and the right column "notes." Underneath the two columns create a box called "summary."

During class, record lecture notes in the "notes" section. In the "keywords" column write down the key words that relate to the group of notes. At home, write a summary of what you have learned in the summary section. To study for a test or quiz, fold your paper between the keywords and notes.

Tips for Taking Good Notes

Not every note-taking style or technique will work for you, so you'll have to develop a system that does. Not matter what style you choose—bulleted, outline, or Cornell—here are some general tips that will make note-taking easier.

Start a New Page Every Day

When taking notes, it's best to start out with a fresh piece of
paper. Be sure to put the date and the lecture topic at the top of
the page where they can be easily spotted later. For those of you
trying to save paper, you can put a thick dividing line at the end
of the previous day's notes and then clearly add the topic and date
below it. Be sure to leave some breathing room so that you can
easily find what you are looking for later.

Leave Blank Spaces

Don't try to use up every square inch of the page. Instead, leave
yourself room to add in information that you might not have
caught the first time, or to write questions or comments that
come up later.

Copy What's on the Board

If your teacher has written something on the board, copy that
down while class is starting up. Most likely it's a brief outline
that will help you keep track of the main points of the lecture
or discussion. This will help you to anticipate what notes you are
going to need to take.

Listen Carefully

Sometimes we worry so much about writing down every word
that the teacher is saying that we forget to listen to what is being
said. Pay attention to what is said and then shorten it into your
own words, rather than trying to record things verbatim. The
more information you're able to capture, the more you are likely
to retain from the lecture.

Use Abbreviations and Symbols

Shorten sentences and words, create symbols, and use abbreviations so that you don't waste unnecessary time writing things out. For example, if your teacher says, "There were three causes of the Civil War," you might write, "3 causes C.W."

You can make up your own library of symbols. Pull from math or science symbols (=,: , > , ^) and texting shorthand (like using np for no problem) to keep your writing to a minimum. Use numbers instead of words. Just don't forget what your symbols mean! Use arrows, lines, boxes, and circles to connect and highlight important ideas.

ADD SOME COLOR

Lots of students find it useful to use different-color pens or highlighters while taking notes. For example, you might want to use one color for the main points and another for the details. Or highlight or underline key terms in a separate color.

Color helps words or ideas pop off the page so that you can easily find what's most important. Warning: Don't use too many different colors. It might look sort of cool, but nothing will end up standing out. So start with two colors.

Pay Attention to Keywords

There are key words and phrases that let you know something important is coming up. We use these in writing but also in speaking to grab the listener's attention. When your teacher says things like, "The main cause of . . . ," "The significance of _____ is . . . ," or "There are three main reasons . . . ," pay attention. Use boxes, different colors, or underlining to make sure this stands out in your notes.

Put It in Your Own Words

Whenever you can, try to write down notes in words that make sense to you. It's okay to use some of the words from the board or directly from your teacher's lecture, but try to make it your own. Translating the ideas into your own words shows you understand them, and helps get that info into your memory. However, when it comes to facts, formulas, or definitions, write down exactly what is presented to you.

Include Examples That Support the Main Ideas

It's important to include the information that helps describe why a main idea is true. It's great to write down the three causes of the Civil War, but to really be able to explain it like you might need to in an essay question on a test you are going to have to give some detail. Use "e.g." or "ex." before the example.

GET CREATIVE

They say a picture is worth a thousand words. So try drawing a picture in your notes instead. Sometimes a diagram explains something more clearly than words do. You can draw what you see on the board or how you see it in your brain. And don't worry about making it museum-worthy. The only person who needs to interpret this piece of art is you.

$\log_a x = \dfrac{\log x}{\log a}$

$\dfrac{(x')^2}{(\sqrt{2})^2} - \dfrac{(y')^2}{(\sqrt{2})^2} = 1$

HERON'S AREA

formula

$Area = \sqrt{s(s-a)(s-b)(s-c)}$

where $s = (a+b+c)/2$

$\cot 2\theta = \dfrac{A-C}{B}$

$\boxed{B \neq 0}$

Receiver

3'

$5 \cos 3\theta$

$\theta' = 72°$

$-72°$

θ'

$2\cos^2 x - 3\cos x + 1 = 0$

$(2\cos x - 1)(\cos x - 1) = 0$

$e = \dfrac{c}{a} \dfrac{(focus)}{(distance)}$

ECCENTRICITY

$b = 27.4 ft$ $102.3°$ a

A c $28.7°$

2

$\dfrac{\pi}{2}$ π $\dfrac{3\pi}{2}$ 2π

PART 3

Studying Smarter

In addition to staying organized, planning ahead, and taking good notes, successful students also have a tendency to not just study harder, but also study smarter. When it comes to studying, they make sure they have a plan and do their work in a place that supports what they are trying to learn. In short, they think about what they're trying to accomplish and work consciously to that end, using the appropriate tools and techniques.

Your time is precious, so use it wisely. Nothing is more frustrating than struggling to think over screaming siblings, or spending time on an assignment only to leave it behind in the morning. If you are willing to put the time in, then you deserve to make the most of it!

Use the tips on the following pages to focus on your work, improve your memory, stay organized, and read more effectively!

Chapter 7
Study Basics

It's really annoying when you don't do well on a test and your teacher says, "Just study harder next time." What if you already tried your hardest and still didn't get the results you wanted? It might be time to examine how you study, from your plan of action to the place you do your work. Here are some basics that every student should learn (but isn't always taught) to help make that study time yield more successful results.

The Right Spot

Finding a quiet place where you can be totally focused on your work is essential to your success in school. If you have a busy schedule, you're probably going to have to finish at least some of your schoolwork on the go, but you should also have a dedicated place to study back at home. To help you maximize your learning potential and optimize the time you spend on your work, it's important to set up a distraction-free area where you can get your work done.

Find Your Study Spot

Some people like total quiet and privacy. Others prefer places like the library, where it's peaceful, but where there's also some ambient noise. And some people can't even begin to study without their iPod! Whether you're focusing intently as you pull together all your notes, or teaching what you're learning to an imaginary student, pick a space that will serve your study needs. The right setup will let you get your work done more efficiently.

While lying on your bed or sitting in front of the TV might be the most comfortable options, it's best to avoid the tempting distraction of *Keeping Up with the Kardashians.* Instead, find a setup that will help you get your work done faster.

Your study spot should have as many of the following qualities as possible. The more the better!

- ❏ Work space that is big enough for you to spread out in
- ❏ Free from interruptions and distractions—far from loud siblings or the TV
- ❏ Available whenever you need to use it
- ❏ Has all the materials you regularly need like binder paper, your schoolbooks, pens, pencils, etc.
- ❏ A comfy chair (but not too comfy!)
- ❏ Good overhead light or a lamp
- ❏ Comfortable temperature
- ❏ Desktop or laptop computer

CREATE A PORTABLE DESK

If you have to share a common space (like a kitchen table) with other people in your house, create your own portable desk. Put all the things that you need for school (such as a pencil sharpener, tape, a stapler, a hole-punch, paper clips, a ruler, Post-its, markers, and glue sticks) into a box and bring it with you. When you're done for the night, load it all back in. The last thing you want is to waste 15 minutes searching for a pencil when you could have gotten through half your problem set in that time. Having the supplies you need at hand is a huge time saver!

Sharpen Your Focus!

How you work is as important as *where* you work. It's tempting to multitask while you do your homework by talking on the phone, tweeting, texting, and signing up for a weekend volunteer gig. While you might feel more productive doing all these tasks at once, it turns out that this isn't always the best approach to learning.

PICKING A STUDY SYMBOL

Sometimes you might need a little boost to get into study mode. Select something that you can wear, listen to, or display only when you study. Consider it a physical theme song that gets you primed and ready to hit the books. Maybe it's your favorite pen, the blanket that your grandma made for you, or a playlist of classical music that helps you concentrate. Whatever it is, only take it out, wear it, or listen to it when you're studying, and it'll help get you focused.

The Truth About Multitasking

Studies have shown that multitasking decreases your ability think critically and gain a deep understanding of what you are trying to learn. When you do several things at once, you're working with the part of the brain that helps you learn repetitive skills, *not* the part that helps you store and recall information. The muscle in your brain that controls your ability to switch back and forth is being developed at the expense of the recall and retention muscle.

Think about it. When you're watching TV and your friend starts to ask you a question, how focused are you on the answer, really?

When you're writing a paper on the computer, texting, and checking TMZ all at the same time, don't you feel like you have to restart your thinking every time you get back to the paper?

TUNES OR NO TUNES?

Anything goes when it comes to your studying soundtrack. Some people find any type of music distracting, while others find it easier to concentrate with music in the background. Or it might be that you can listen to any kind of music while you do math, but can only listen to instrumental music when you're reading or writing. The part of the brain that does word processing and is used for studying is the same part that listens to song lyrics. Pay attention to what works and what you find distracting so you can create the ideal study atmosphere for each subject.

We live in a busy world, and it's not very realistic to expect to stop multitasking altogether. But how do you decide when to focus and when to spread your attention around?

First and foremost: Be thoughtful about your multitasking. For high-priority and challenging assignments—the really tough stuff—make sure you're paying close attention to that assignment and nothing else. Get away from any potential distractions. Put your phone in another room, and log out of chat, Facebook, and any other apps that are unrelated to what you're doing. (They'll eventually make your study break that much sweeter.)

On the other hand, for assignments that take less brainpower or are less important, sending those occasional texts to your BFF shouldn't take you too far off task.

Make a Study Plan

If you have a major test coming up, take 5-10 minutes to put together a quick plan of action. A clear study plan will help you manage your schedule and ensure that you have enough time to fully prepare for your exam.

But how much time do you really need to budget for each individual test? The answer depends on how important the test is, what you need to know, and how much time you have. If it's an important test that will have a big effect on your grade, be sure to budget plenty of time. A major task like that can easily take two hours a night for a week. On the other hand, if the test won't have much of an impact on your grade or you know the material super well, you may just need a quick review.

Set a Goal

Figure out what your goal grade is for the test. Depending on how you have done on past work and how important this test is to your overall grade, set a goal for yourself and make sure it's SMART. (See pages 12-13.)

Start Early and Space Out Your Study Sessions

The earlier you start to review, the better you will learn the material, because you won't be trying to jam it all into your brain at once. Cramming the events of the entire Russian Revolution into your head on two hours of sleep will most likely leave you exhausted, with only a few scraps of information that really stick. Ideally, you want to be able to have multiple study sessions over a couple of weeks. Use the timetable mentioned before: around 45 minutes of studying and 15 minutes of break time per hour. If you only have time to study on the weekends, try to spread the hours out across the two days.

TIME SAVER: TAKE BREAKS (NO, REALLY)

It's admirable to set aside four hours on a weekend to study for your physics final, but make sure you take a break every hour or so to give yourself a chance to rejuvenate. If you're doing a marathon study session, consider breaking it up into two shorter sessions and taking a longer break in between. Go for a run, listen to your favorite music, play with your dog. Your brain needs time to recharge—and you'll absorb that much more when you do get back to the books.

Remember the weekly schedule from Chapter 2? Use the same principle to block out chunks of time that you can devote to studying. Think about your daily commitments as well as your regular homework load. Once you've blocked off the time, take out your study guide and break it down into several parts. Assign different parts to each study session, starting with the material that needs the most work. Leave yourself a few sessions at the end to do a general review of everything.

United States History Final Study Plan

	Monday	Tuesday	Wednesday	Thursday	Friday	Saturday
Week One	Gilded Age	Progressive Era	Imperialism	1920s		Great Depression
Week Two		Review Gilded Age and Progressive Era	Review Imperialism, 1920s, and Great Depression	Review all	TEST	

A Note on Memory

Memory is a tricky business: The information stored in our brains doesn't have an automatic expiration date, and some things will stick around with almost no conscious effort, while other things seem determined to flutter, no matter what. Memory takes work; it requires maintenance. But with that being said, there are some basic things we can do to help keep our mental storage lockers in good working order so that we can find what we need when we need it.

Strategy #1: Sleep!

The first thing you should focus on (and, in a way, the easiest issue to address) is sleep. Sleep allows your brain to sort through the things you've learned and experienced in the course of the day—and without a good night's rest, you're always going to struggle. So do yourself a favor, and go to sleep!

Strategy #2: Be an active listener

In the course of your school day the very act of listening and learning is going to act as the greatest aid to comprehension and retention. So pay attention in class, try not to multitask, and, as we discussed earlier, do your best to engage with the material in a constructive way.

Strategy #3: Make connections

Speaking of constructive participation, it's also important to try and connect what you're learning to something you already know. You might even want to check in on this issue once or twice a class, and force yourself to finish the sentence: "This reminds me of..." Your memory is enhanced when you make associations to what's already stored on your mental hard drive.

Strategy #4: Practice

When you get home, get right down to business and practice, practice, practice. Reinforce what you've learned by doing problems, repeating the material out loud, teaching it to other people, rephrasing the text in front of you, and rereading whatever was confusing. This helps move the information from your short-term memory over to your permanent memory, and also makes sure that you can recall it when you need it.

Study Groups: Divide and Conquer

There's strength in numbers! Study groups offer a tried-and-true way of learning material faster and more completely. Study groups aren't for everyone—they do require some extra coordination and preparation—but if you can fit it into your schedule and find the right people, working with a study group can have some terrific benefits. By engaging with your homework through discussion, explanation, and debate, you'll gain a much more thorough understanding of the material.

The ideal group is made up of, say, three to five people with similar goals and a range of skills and talents. Groups that meet on the same day and at the same time each week find they get better participation. If you find you can't get a whole group together, or if there's one person that you tend to work well with, having a single study buddy can also make a big difference, because you'll be able to encourage and support one another as you work.

You can work with a group to study for a class in general or just for a particularly difficult exam. It's up to you! But once you get started it will be hard to go back, because the benefits are huge. Let us count the ways…

> ## STUDY-GROUP TIPS
>
> While study groups can be immensely helpful, it is possible to have a little *too* much fun. Stay on track by making sure you have goals for each session and that group members prepare in advance. This means doing the reading or bringing notes. You don't want to spend your group work time waiting for one person to get caught up.
>
> Determine how long you will meet for each session—if it's two hours or more, be sure to take a break in between. Make one person the group facilitator who keeps track of time and gets the group on task.

Socializing!

Having other people around makes studying more interactive and fun. Multiple group members provide the opportunity to quiz one another, compare notes and assignments, and reap the benefits of bouncing ideas off of different people. Besides, sitting alone for hours on end is really boring!

A Shorter Learning Curve

You can learn faster and cover more ground in a study group. Someone in the group might be able to explain something much more quickly than you might have figured it out on your own. Or together the group might solve a complicated problem that no one could do solo. You can also break up the work—individual members can become "experts" on a certain part of the material and teach the rest of the group what they need to know.

Decreased Likelihood of Procrastination

Study groups are excellent procrastination-busters. As an integral part of a group, you're more likely to actually take responsibility for your work. And because the group meets at a certain time on a certain day, you can't just wait until the last minute to get your studying done. The rest of the team depends on you!

Math 101

Studying for math is a bit different. Unlike many other subjects, math relies heavily on your past experience and knowledge. The more that you understand what you are learning today, the more it will help you tomorrow. And in order to really get what you are doing today, you need to (1) understand the concept the teacher is presenting, and (2) practice, practice, practice.

Understand the Concepts

In most math classes, the teacher will present you with a new math concept and then show you a bunch of different ways to solve problems using that technique or formula. Sometimes you follow along and totally get it. Other times, the explanation sounds like gibberish in the first place, so when your teacher is going through the problems, nothing is really adding up, so to speak. Afterward, you'll probably do some problems in class or be assigned some for homework, and that's where things can get dicey. Here's a quick rundown of two common scenarios, along with advice about how to address them.

Scenario 1: But I understood it in class!

Situation: During geometry today, you had no problem understanding how to find the midpoint. Your teacher's explanation made perfect sense, so you didn't feel the need to write down all the steps. And those practice problems in class?

Piece of cake. But when you get home from school, what made total sense in class is no longer clear.

Insider tip: Sometimes when things are explained to us they make sense and we can apply that knowledge right away. But if you've had many hours between math and the time you are doing your homework, then you might forget a key step or explanation that makes it all come together.

Solution: Write down the entire process so that you can go back and re-create the steps that made perfect sense earlier in the day. It will make it that much easier to refresh your memory hours later.

Scenario 2: I just don't get how to do it

Situation: During algebra your teacher went over multiplying polynomials using the area model... but she might as well have been speaking another language. The explanation just didn't make any sense to you, and when she started talking about breaking the problem into different rectangles, she lost you completely.

Insider tip: Sometimes the way the teacher explains something doesn't always make sense the first time. She might be using terms that you don't know, or you might have spaced out for a moment and missed a critical piece.

Solution: It doesn't matter why you didn't get it, it just matters that you didn't get it. You have several ways to get an explanation that makes sense. First, reread your notes. Sometimes you can figure things out by walking yourself back through the process. If things still don't make sense, you're going to need to find a way to get things re-explained in a way that you can understand. Get help from your teacher, seek help from a tutor, ask a friend in class, or check out some of the resources found on the internet. There are some that specialize in math help, like Khan Academy, or you can search for videos on YouTube. Lots of teachers these days are putting up math videos to help students outside the classroom.

Practice, Practice, Practice

Because each math lesson builds on the one before, it's critical that you stay on top of your work. Practice each new concept you learn by doing problems in class and at home. That way, you'll arrive prepared and will be able to get a lot out of every class, which will help you practice more concepts, which will help you arrive prepared… You get the picture.

If you find yourself struggling with some of the homework, try using your resources—friends, math videos, textbooks—to help you to understand it. If you still don't get it, circle the problem and go in early the next day to discuss it with your teacher.

Do Your Work Every Day

Some teachers allow you to turn in your assignments at the end of a week or unit. While this seems like a great opportunity to put your assignments off until the last minute, don't! If you complete assignments before your next class, the next concept you learn will make way more sense. And—the real bonus—you won't have to complete a week's worth of assignments on the night before they're due.

Chapter 8
Getting Organized

Organization isn't necessarily something that you're taught in school, but it's one of the secrets to academic success. If you can't imagine anything more enjoyable than color-coding and labeling everything, you were probably born with that organization gene. For everyone else, there's a natural tendency to throw everything in a backpack, zip it up, and hope it doesn't explode. For those not organizationally inclined, here's some good news: There are some simple systems that can transform your organizational challenges into victories.

Start by picking the right tool, and then organize your papers and computer files so that whatever you need will be a mouse click or fingertip away.

Choose Your Tool

With the huge amount of books, homework, and handouts that you have for every class, keeping track of it all can sometimes feel like a lost cause. But finding a way to keep all of your papers and projects organized is a must for both your grades and your peace of mind.

There are lots of different tools out there for managing all of your paper. Sometimes your teacher will tell you what he wants you to use. But if it's your choice, here are the top tools for managing and organizing your school stuff.

Option #1: The Three-Ring Binder

Ideal for . . .

Classes that have tons of paper, like a science class, where you get lots of handouts and take pages of notes.

How it works

The three-ring-binder uses color-tabbed dividers to show where everything goes, and a three-hole punch to make all of your handouts binder-friendly. Depending on the size of your binder and the amount of space that you need, you can either use one binder per class or double up.

DON'T FORGET TO DATE

Write the date in the top right-hand corner of all handouts, homework assignments, returned tests, and any other course-work. This helps keep your papers in order, and makes it easier to see if something's missing.

Use your color-tabbed dividers to sort papers into the five sections listed below. ("The Right Sort," on page 96, will explain what each section is for.)

Tab #1: To Do

Tab #2: Current Topic

Tab #3: Past Topics & Returned Tests/Essays

Tab #4: Reference

Tab #5: Paper (keep fully stocked)

(In addition to these five, feel free to make other categories custom-tailored to each class, like a "Vocab" section for English, or a "Lab" section for Biology.)

Tip
Keep all completed homework in the front pocket or a plastic sleeve. This way you never have to dig around, and it won't get crumpled up or lost. Throughout the day, add handouts or assignments to the front pocket or sleeve. Later on, move them into the proper tab in your binder.

Beware
The front pocket of your binder will get full fast. To cut down on clutter, take a few minutes every night to file away those random papers under the correct tab.

Option #2: The Accordion File

Ideal for . . .
Classes with a medium amount of note-taking and handouts.

How it works
An accordion file is a stretchable folder that's divided into tabbed sections. Like the binder system mentioned earlier, this setup allows you to sort papers by type. Depending on the size and the amount of space you need, each class can get its own file, or multiple classes can share one.

Accordion files are great because they keep everything sorted and don't require a three-hole punch. Depending on how many you use and how full they are, they can be less bulky and fit in a backpack more easily than three-ring binders. Using accordion files also eliminates the need for additional pocket folders. It's best to use a flap-top accordion file that closes securely with Velcro or an elastic band.

If you are using one accordion file per class, sort your papers into the following five sections—one for each tab. (See "The Right Sort," on page 96, for more info on what each section is for.)

Tab #1: To Do

Tab #2: Current Topic

Tab #3: Past Topics & Returned Tests/Essays

Tab #4: Reference

Tab #5: Paper (keep fully stocked)

(Some students like to use an accordion file to keep all the homework assignments they are turning in for each class organized, instead of using one accordian file for each class. If you choose this method, just label each tab with the name of the class)

Tips

When you finish your homework at night, put the completed assignments into the corresponding slots.

Any time you get a handout or returned work in class, immediately put it in its place so that everything stays sorted.

Beware

Unlike binders and notebooks, accordion files allow you to stow papers out of sight, which makes it easy to forget what's in there. To avoid overstuffed files and keep this system running smoothly, take a few minutes every week to clear out anything you don't need, and to reorganize the stuff that you do want.

TIME SAVER: COLOR CODING

One way to make your least favorite subjects a little more appetizing is to give them some color. So in other words, if you dread opening up to your calculus homework, connect it with your favorite color (fire-engine red, perhaps!). And once you pick that color, assign it to everything in that class—binder, folders, files, and so on. When every class is coded a different color, it's easy to grab exactly what you need.

Option #3: The Spiral Notebook System

Ideal for . . .

Classes where the teacher asks for an interactive notebook, or any class that's relatively light on handouts but heavy on note-taking.

How it works

Use spiral notebooks for selected classes. In a spiral notebook, you keep everything from class notes to homework assignments arranged in chronological order. This method works well if a teacher prefers spiral notebooks to binders, or if you tend to remember things by date (like for instance, that you read *The Good Earth* in May, and *The Great Gatsby* in April) instead of by type (homework, class work, tests, etc.). Spiral notebooks are also less bulky than either binders or accordion files, and can be more comfortable to write in. Notebook paper also won't fall out as easily as binder paper, so you're less likely to have floaters roaming around your backpack.

With a spiral notebook, everything is automatically kept in chronological order. (But make sure you still put dates on all of your work, because that's how you'll find it again later!) Attach—using a glue stick, staples, tape, or a chewing-gum wad—class calendars and handouts directly to the notebook as soon as you get them.

Anything that can't or shouldn't be attached to a sheet of paper in the spiral notebook—like double-sided or multipage handouts, returned tests, or assignments to hand in—goes into a folder, color-coded to match the notebook from that same class.

Tips

If you use spiral notebooks for all of your classes, you might want to try using an accordion file or folder to store the extra papers from each class.

If you're using a two-pocket folder, put current handouts in the left-side pocket and past ones on the right.

Try to always have a glue stick or stapler handy to attach rogue handouts and other papers to the pages of your notebook.

Beware

Glue and staple carefully! You don't want the pages to stick together or get too bulky. Keeping everything in spiral notebooks requires daily maintenance: Make sure you do regular upkeep if you choose this method. (If you're at all on the sloppy side . . . this may not be the best system for you.)

The Right Sort

If you chose the three-ring binder or accordion file for any of your subjects, then you had to make five sections for each class. Now let's talk about what to put in those sections. You'll also learn to use a file box, which is handy even if you chose the spiral notebook for all of your classes.

From term papers to pop quizzes, all of your papers will fall into one of the four categories below:

To Do

Anything you have not done yet (that's why it's "to do"!), including papers that relate to assignments, worksheets, upcoming tests or quizzes, or readings you'll do outside of class.

Current Topic

Any materials related to the topic you're currently studying in class such as notes, articles, completed worksheets, and graded homework assignments

ESSENTIAL SKILLS: STICKING WITH IT

No matter what system you pick, the key to keeping it going is to file away each item as soon as you get it in your hands. This way you can skirt the law of nature that says your most important papers will inevitably end up lost, trampled, or stuck together.

Past Topics & Returned Tests/Essays

Any papers relating to the previous topics you've covered in class. These can be returned tests or assignments, worksheets, reading materials, or anything else that you covered previously (biology notes about the worm that you disected, for instance). And, again, keep them in chronological order—oldest to newest.

Reference

Any calendars, syllabi, participation rubrics, "how-to" sheets, reference lists, or other one-shot-deal papers that you might need for reference throughout the semester. If your teacher said, "Don't lose this—you're only getting it once," then it belongs in Reference!

ORGANIZING YOUR MATERIALS

Over the course of a unit, it's easy for your materials to become disorganized or separated from each other. Putting your papers in chronological order ensures that everything you need is right at your fingertips. In your binder or a folder, put together all of your class notes, handouts, and homework and organize them by date, from oldest to newest. For each topic, put the class notes and handouts first, followed by the prac-tice problems or related homework. If you have any tests or quizzes, put those after the practice problems. You might want to paper-clip each topic or section together or label it with a Post-it for easy identification.

Your File Box

A file box is like your own miniature filing cabinet. Plastic, wooden, or metal, it sits on or near your desk and allows you to keep files at your fingertips. Use it in these two ways:

Store Past Units of Work

Once the "Past Topics & Returned Tests/Essays" section of your binder or accordion file gets full or outdated, you'll need to move that stuff into a new place. This is where the file box comes in. Make a file for each class and put the overflow here.

TIME-SAVER: THE MONTHLY SWEEP

Make a half-hour date with yourself once a month to go through your stuff and get rid of whatever you don't need. Extra clutter adds unnecessary weight to your backpack and only gets in the way. This monthly sweep is also a good time to sort any loose papers that need a home (returned trig home-work, notes to your former crush, frame-worthy doodles), and just to neaten things up in general. Put your cleanup date in your planner.

Saving Papers You Will Need for Later

The file box is also the perfect place to put other random papers and flat stuff that you don't have a home for, whether it's an end-of-the year portfolio for English, future college applications, letters of recommendation from teachers, or your driver's ed. certificate. You can even file that ribbon you won for best origami butterfly here. (What, you don't want to frame that?)

To keep your system streamlined, go through the file box once a month to get rid of anything you don't need anymore.

TIME-SAVER: THE MUST HAVE LIST

Good organization lets you get things done the way you need to—but to do that, you need the right tools. Here's a list of things that every student should have at his or her disposal:

- A planner (electronic or paper)
- Pencils and pens (preferably in a pencil bag of some sort)
- Sticky notes or mini writing pad
- Highlighters
- Calculator
- Mini stapler
- Scotch tape
- A USB memory stick (for backing up electronic files)

Your Digital Desktop: Keep Computer Files Organized

All of this paper sorting won't do any good if your computer is still in disarray. Organizing digital files is just as important as the other stuff—especially if you do most of your homework on-screen. Try this method to keep your computer in order and your digital files easy to find.

School Folder

Create a folder on your hard drive for all school-related stuff. To lighten things up, give it a fun nickname that makes it clear that it belongs to you (and not your weird cousin who always uses your computer when he visits). Then create a shortcut icon on your desktop so you can get to your stuff fast.

Grade folders

Make one folder for each year of school (10th grade, 11th grade, etc.) and put them in the main folder.

2 POCKET FOLDER

Class folders

Within the grade folder, create separate folders for each subject you're taking (English, Astronomy, etc.).

Topic folders

Add subfolders within each class folder for the key topics that you're studying, like "World War I" for History, or *"Macbeth"* for English.

TIME SAVER: "SAVE AS"

If you're working on a second draft of a paper or project, don't save over the original. Instead, do a "save as" and name the versions "Macbeth_essay_1," "Macbeth_essay_2," and so on. That way, if something happens to the new file, you won't have to start from scratch. You also have the option of reverting to the original version if you decide you liked it better.

Back It Up and Bring It Along

You probably know by now that having a good system for transporting digital files from one place to the next is a total necessity. If you start a project on another computer at school, the library, or a friend's house, you need a quick, reliable way to get your document home, or vice versa.

Backing stuff up is also super important. If you're like most people, your life is on your computer. That makes losing your hard drive due to theft or system error a very scary thought. Protect your files (and your sanity) by backing up all of your important docs at least once every two weeks. That way, if you lose something on your computer, all the brilliant work you've done won't just go "poof"!

You have lots of choices for how to access your docs when you need them. The chart on the following page shows different ways to both transfer and back up your files.

LEAVE A PAPER TRAIL

It's also helpful to print out new files and keep these printouts somewhere in your file box. It might seem like overkill now, but when you lose the computer file for that 20-page masterpiece on Queen Nefertiti, it will be a huge relief to find a printout safe and sound in your file box. Sure, you may need to retype it, but at least you won't need to *rewrite it.*

Tool	Description	Transfer	Back it up
E-mail	Send the document to yourself as an attachment. (I always like this method because it's fast, reliable, and free.)	x	
The "cloud"	Sign up with an online server like dropbox.com, iCloud, or box.net that will let you drag and drop files to store on the web for free. You can use this to save files from school that you use at home and as a way to store your files in the "cloud" so that you can access what you need no matter where you are (as long as you are connected to the internet).	x	x
USB drive	Use a USB memory stick, which lets you save files in one place and then transfer them to your own hard drive later (just make sure the memory stick is compatible with both machines). Memory sticks are affordable and easy to use, but they're also small and can get lost easily. If you're using one, put your name on it and keep it in an inside pocket of your backpack where it will be safe from damage or loss.	x	x
External hard drive	Use this handy little gizmo to back up everything on your computer's internal hard drive.		x

Chapter 9
The Right Read

By the time you're in high school, you're probably spending more time reading textbooks and articles than anything else. Novels are no longer entertainment, but rather "texts" that you interpret or analyze. For many classes, reading plays a large part in how you learn about the subject, and much of your homework includes reading and some sort of writing assignment. Are you looking for information, trying to understand something new, seeking to gain a deeper meaning, or just reading for fun?

Now that reading is more about analysis than enjoyment, you'll want to shift the way in which you approach your task. Successful students use a variety of different techniques to discover the meaning in what they are reading. To choose the right technique, take a moment to figure out *why* you are being asked to read something.

Reading Techniques

Choosing the right reading techniques will not only save you time but also help you get the job done right. For most types of reading, you will use many different methods. These techniques should become like gears on a bicycle: You'll eventually learn to shift in and out of them without thinking about it as you go up and down the hills. So let's start out by identifying these "gears"…

Pre-reading

Pre-reading only takes a few moments. It helps you shift your head into the right mindset and primes you for what you are about to learn. There are two quick steps to pre-reading: connecting what you are about to learn to what you already know, and previewing the material to get a better sense of the overall message.

Connect to what you know

Before you start reading, think about the assignment topic. Ask yourself, "What do I already know about this topic?" It could be what you talked about in class, or even something that you learned last year. Then ask yourself, "What do I hope to learn now?" By asking yourself these questions, you prime your brain for the topic at hand, and become more curious and engaged—a critical step in learning new information.

Preview the material

Take a minute or so to preview the material you are about to read. Consider this process like a quick tour of the area, so that you know what the overall discussion "looks like," and learn where everything is located. Use the following steps to identify main ideas and key terms:

Find the main topic

Focus in on the title and subtitle of the chapter so that you emphasize the main topic in your own head.

Identify the main ideas

Read both the introduction and the conclusion so you understand what the main ideas are and why they are important. Glance through the chapter and read the section titles, words in bold or italics, and any questions that are noted in the margins. (If you have an assignment that asks you to identify and explain keywords, previewing the material can help you locate them.)

Scan the chapter

Scan the chapter for graphs, images, maps, and illustrations. Spend five to ten seconds looking at each one, and think about the story these images are telling you.

Active Reading

Active reading is all about knowing why you are reading something and then interacting with the material while you read so that you understand and remember it better. It might seem easier and faster just to let the words sort of float through your head, but the message doesn't stick nearly as well with that kind of passive reading.

With active reading, you pose questions, make predictions, look for clarification, identify keywords or sections that you think provide key points, and paraphrase what you have read into your own words. Often this means highlighting or underlining text or taking notes—just doing something to ensure that you are engaging in a running dialog with the text. The more you interact with what you read, the more you will retain and understand the given material.

You can use the following guidelines to start reading more actively.

Find connections

Active reading works best after you've already familiarized yourself with the text via a pre-read, but even when you begin this deeper, more active stage of reading, it's worth taking a step back periodically to ask yourself, as you did before, how what you're learning now relates to what you've learned previously. Make those connections, and your memory will thank you later.

Mark it up

You should have a pencil and Post-its nearby so that you can underline or make a note of any passages or terms that you might need additional help with. Take notes on things that you think are particularly important, explaining why they matter so much, and how they relate to the rest of the material. When there's a key idea that you want to remember, make a note to yourself, and explain the concept in your own words.

Reread the confusing stuff

Once you've finished reading, take a second look at anything that was confusing (which you should have already marked out for review). You can skim over sections that you already understand. Sometimes you might need to go back over things more than once, and that's okay since it's better than just rushing through it and not actually learning the material.

Sum it up

When you're done, summarize what you've read. It's a great way to see if you really learned the material.

Scan Versus Skim

Both skimming and scanning are fast reading techniques that will help you review material without reading every word. But they do so in different ways with different outcomes.

Scanning

Scanning is when you very quickly look through a document for specific information and then read that info very carefully. You are not trying to understand all the words on the page, only those that pertain to your search. For example, you would scan an index or table of contents for a particular word.

Tips for scanning: Identify what you are searching for and keep that in mind (it's easy to get distracted!).

- Use headings to help guide your search.

- Skip irrelevant sections.

- Look for words in bold and italics.

- Run your finger across the text to help look for the words you are searching for.

- Allow your eyes to across move across several lines of print at once.

- When you find what you're looking for, slow down and start reading at your normal rate.

Skimming

Skimming is when you read over a section quickly, with the purpose of answering a particular question or identifying the most important points of the discussion. For example, when doing research you skim an article to find out if it has the information you are seeking. But you shouldn't ever be skimming over an entire assignment: You'll need to stop and slow down when you hit important or dense sections of text.

Skimming is especially useful when you want to review something you've already read or when you just need some quick information.

Tips for skimming: Carefully read the title, introduction, and first paragraph completely.

- Read the topic sentence of each paragraph. Then, move your eyes quickly, looking for clue words that answer who, what, when, where, and how. Use your finger to focus your eyes and keep track of where you are.

- Be on the lookout for words such as causes, effects, results, pro, and con, and words that are bold or in italics.

- Read headings and subheadings and pay attention to pictures, graphs, charts, and illustrations.

- Read the last paragraph carefully.

Tackling the Textbook

Textbooks can be daunting and boring all at once. Often they are dense and dry and, well, just not very interesting. So how do you stay awake, keep focused, and get the most out of what you are reading?

Survey

Before you read, survey or pre-read the chapter's title, heading, and subheadings. Look at the pictures, charts, graphs, and maps, and read the captions underneath. Read the introduction and conclusion. This will give you a good sense of what the chapter is about and help you know what you're looking for.

Question

As you read, seek to answer questions you have about the material. If you don't have any questions of your own, check out the end-of-chapter questions in the text, or turn the subheadings into questions. You can also draw on what your teacher asked in class, or your homework assignment. When you question as you read, it increases your concentration and helps you focus on what you need to get out of the reading.

Read

Read the material, looking for answers to your questions, and take notes to help you remember them, making sure to include important details and key terms. Take another look at the illustrations and graphs and reread the captions. Slow down when things don't make sense and reread sections if they aren't clear.

Recite

After each section, summarize what you've learned by reciting it out loud. This lets you keep what you've learned in check and helps things stick in your long-term memory. Make a note of things that you couldn't remember.

Connect

Here again, it's important to make connections and find some glue to make these new concepts and ideas stick. Making personal connections is a great way to get new information into your long-term memory.

Review

After you've finished the reading, skim back over the chapter and read your notes. Quiz yourself out loud using the questions that you came up with at the beginning. Summarize the information by making a concept map (see page 118), writing up a summary, or drawing a flowchart or graphic.

PART 4

Testing Things Out

Tests are stressful—but they don't have to be. With the right preparation you can go into the test feeling cool, confident, and relaxed (well, relatively relaxed). But proper preparation takes real planning. This final section of the book provides a rundown of everything you need to know to get organized, study more efficiently, and perform better on tests.

Remember, good prep starts way before the exam. Test taking becomes much more manageable if you apply yourself throughout the semester, rather than just at the end. In class, this means paying attention, taking notes, and asking good questions. Out of class, it means really focusing on your work and following up on things that just don't make sense. If you get an assignment or quiz back and see a string of wrong answers, take the time to correct those and learn from your mistakes. In other words, do everything you've just read about in this book!

If you use these tips on a daily basis, you won't have to freak out during crunch time. The overall goal, come test time, is for you to be able to simply apply what you've absorbed over time (and reinforced in the closing days), instead of having to cram everything in at the last minute and scrambling to recover that mass of information at the critical moment. So without further ado, let's talk tests!

Chapter 10
What to Learn and How to Learn It

Test-taking skills are critical to high school success, but very few teachers actually provide their students with the guidance they need to study effectively for tests in general. Teacher-provided study guides and in-class review sessions are great and very helpful, but students also need to learn how to identify what matters, absorb what's important, and organize their material in a way that supports and supplements their studying habits.

Given that studying takes so much time, you want to make sure that you're spending your time on the things that really matter, and applying yourself in the most effective way possible. That's what we'll be focusing on now: the key aspects of test preparation.

Identify What You Need to Learn

For every test, you need to first make sure that you know exactly what it is you need to study. Creating a study guide (a list of terms and concepts you need to learn) can help you focus your time and efforts, and determine what areas need the most attention. And as with the SMART goals we discussed earlier, the more specific you can be about your goals and responsibilities, the better.

Some teachers provide study guides. In that case, you'll have received a real head start, but if no such guide is provided, you'll have to make one.

> **MAKING YOUR STUDY GUIDE MORE USER-FRIENDLY**
>
> Sometimes the information in the study guide you get from your teacher is put into alphabetical order rather than organized by chapter, topic, or concept. If that's not what you're looking for, you don't have to muddle through with a study guide that isn't working for you. Reorganize it! Figure out what the different categories would be and create your own list, placing the terms into the appropriate category. This creates families of information and helps you remember the relationships between the terms. And, because you're making associations, you're more likely to remember the material!

How to Make Your Own Study Guide

The best thing about making your own guide is the fact that the process itself—going through the materials and identifying what's important—also acts as an aid to the overall learning process. So while it might seem like a little extra work, you are actually enhancing your study process by putting it together. To make your own guide, follow these two steps:

1. Gather and organize

Gather and organize your resources. Pull out your textbook, your class notes, homework, and any quizzes or tests you have already taken. Take a few minutes to organize the information by date. Then grab a piece of paper or open up a new Word document, because now it's time for step two...

2. Create your list

A study guide is not a comprehensive listing of everything that was covered in the course, but rather, a curated collection of the most relevant topics and terms. Think about what sections were covered in great detail and address those first. If you spent two full classes learning about the causes of World War I, there's a good chance that topic will be covered on the exam in some detail. On the other hand, if your teacher didn't focus on any of the battles, you probably don't need to worry about learning them now. Another way of thinking about what you have to learn is to imagine yourself teaching the material you have learned to a 5th grader. What are the three to five key things you would share?

Start by skimming through the relevant textbook chapters, class notes, homework assignments, handouts, and returned quizzes to identify the key concepts, terms, ideas, or types of problems that were covered in the unit. Write them down as you go. If you think that the topic is super important or you don't remember much about it, bold it or put a star next to it so you remember to review those first.

Sample Study Guide

○	**Reconstructing the South**
	"Swing around the circle"
	Reconstruction Acts *
○	Impeachment of Andrew Johnson
	15th Amendment *
	Carpetbaggers and scalawags
	KKK
	Enforcement Acts
○	

Learning Concepts

After you've created your study guide and figured out exactly what topics, keywords, practice problems, or essay prompts will be included on the test, you can then move on to the actual studying—and now you don't have to worry about getting off track or wasting your time! Later in this chapter we'll talk more specifically about some memorization tips and strategies, but before attempting to nail down the details, it's worth taking a step back and attempting to get your head around the concepts first. After all, it's one thing to memorize the quadratic equation, but it's another thing entirely to know how to use it. This is why understanding concepts is so important: When you gain an understanding of an overarching concept, you not only put the individual ideas into context, but also find a means of making new connections between them.

The best way to learn concepts is to figure out how the different terms and ideas all relate to each other. There are two types of study tools that can help you find these relationships: (1) study notes (which can be built directly out of your study guide), and (2) concept maps. Both tools work equally well, so try them out and use the one that suits your style the best.

How to Turn Your Study Guide into Study Notes

Study notes cover all the same topics that are included in the study guide, but use class notes, handouts, textbooks, and past homework assignments to go into much more detail. This doesn't mean re-copying everything word for word, but rather taking the key information and putting it into one document. The process of transferring the information from one place to another actually helps you learn the material better. And because you are paraphrasing or summarizing the information rather than just copying words, the material tends to stick a little bit better.

Here's how to create your own study notes:

Take out your study guide (either the one you made for yourself or the one your teacher gave you), and follow these three easy steps to turn it into study notes.

1. Grab all of your study materials: class notes, handouts, homework, quizzes, and textbooks.

2. Review the material. Start at the beginning of the study guide and work your way through absolutely everything that's included there. Use your skimming skills to re-familiarize yourself with the key terms and concepts.

3. Create your notes by organizing the guide into main ideas and supporting details. (Study notes are not a list of the items you need to learn with definitions, but rather an explanation of ideas and concepts using supporting details.) Use indenting and white space to help you recognize the main idea and supporting details (See "Different Types of Notes," page 66) for each of the topics.

As you review the material, think about how much you really understand and how much is confusing. If you're able to explain the concepts and key terms in writing or out loud (without peeking at your notes), then you won't need to spend as much time learning them later on.

Reconstructing the South

"Swing around the circle"

- Johnson goes on speaking tour of the Midwest and has shouting match with audiences—slams radicals
- 1866 Congressional elections—Republicans win 2/3 majority

Reconstruction Acts—Conditions under which Southern state governments are formed:

- Military Reconstruction Act

  To block obstruction by president

- Command of Army Act
- Tenure of Office Act

Impeachment—Andrew Johnson

- Used Tenure of Office Act to impeach
- Johnson well-behaved during trials
- Failure to remove pres. damages both rep. morale & support
  - Horace Greeley, *New York Times* editor, called Johnson, "an aching in the tooth of the national jaw, a screeching infant in a crowded lecture room. There can be no peace or comfort till he is out."

15th Amendment

- Forbade any citizen from being denied the right to vote on grounds of race, color, or previous condition of servitude.
  - Women wanted to be included on this— but were omitted

Carpetbaggers and scalawags

- Carpetbaggers—Northern pol. opportunists helping with the reconstruction process
- Scalawags—Southern white Republicans (HATED!)

KKK—Organized 1866

- Harassed blacks—wanted to scare them away from voting
- Lynched blacks and disliked politicians

Enforcement Acts (1870-71)

- Penalties for people who interfered w/citizens' right to vote
- Supervised election of congressmen
- Outlawed Klan-type activities
  - 1871 — Fed. Gov. singled out Klan heavy counties activity
    - Pursued mass prosecution
    - HALTED Klan terrorism

How to create a concept map

A concept map is essentially your study notes (and you should absolutely make use of your study guide in creating your concept map), but a concept map places a greater emphasis on the relationships between different topics or ideas. Your concept map begins with a subject, concept, or unit (placed in a circle or square in the center of your paper), and then branches out to cover the main ideas and key details that are related to that concept. Each sub-idea is surrounded by branches of supporting details connected by lines or arrows showing relationships between the items. The process of transforming your notes, handouts, and textbook material into a new, more visual format helps you to see the connections, and helps your brain to absorb the material.

Sample Concept Map

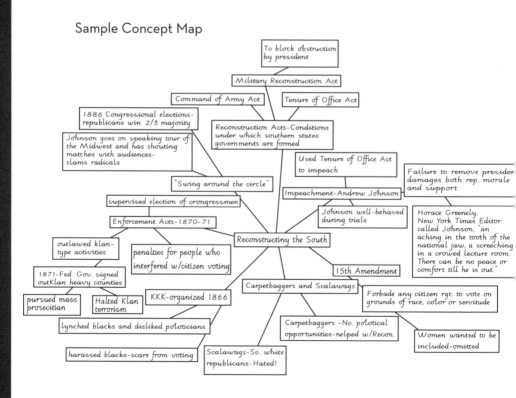

Learn the Material

Now that you've figured out what you need to know and begun to comprehend the concepts, it's time to roll up your sleeves and get down to brass tacks. You should start by conducting a thorough review of the material and then spend the rest of your time testing yourself, or creating study devices that will help move the information from your books and notes into your brain.

Depending on the type of test, you will need to show that you've either memorized or understand the material in question. (Sometimes, of course, you may have to do both.) Pick the best study technique that's most appropriate for the manner in which you are going to be tested. And if you don't know which is appropriate, then ask!

CRITICAL QUESTION: HOW MUCH DOES THIS COUNT TOWARD MY FINAL GRADE?

Ideally, you want to do well on all of your exams. That being said, there are times when getting that top grade will have a minimal effect on your final grade in one class, but will have a huge impact in another. If you find yourself in this situation, make sure you put your eggs in the right basket. If the "A" is not going to have a big impact on your overall grade in the one class, learn the big pieces and then spend your extra time on the material that will make the difference in the other class.

Memorization Techniques

While memorizing takes time and effort, there isn't much in the way of mental gymnastics going on, so it's actually pretty easy.

There are two main ways to help put that material into your memory: (1) mnemonic devices and (2) flash cards.

1. Mnemonic devices

Mnemonic devices are memory aids that help you consolidate information into something that is easier for you to remember. (The word *mnemonic* derives from the name of the goddess of memory in Greek mythology, Mnemosyne.) Mnemonic devices include songs, rhymes, poems, sentences, expressions, or a series of associations that help to trigger your memory. Basically, you associate the thing you are trying to remember with something that is already familiar.

The more you connect something you are learning to something you already know, the easier it will be for that information to become permanent in your memory. The idea is that the more familiar item—which you are way less likely to forget—triggers the connection in your brain to the more foreign concept, making it easier for you to recall lists, parts, names, or steps in a complicated process.

Below are descriptions and examples of three main types of mnemonic devices—acronyms, acrostics, and songs—along with a discussion of flash cards as well.

Acronyms
Ideal for: Remembering short lists (seven things or fewer) or an order of operation.

An acronym is an invented combination of letters that forms a new "word" that stands for something else. Each letter is your clue. For example, PEMDAS (Parenthesis, Exponents, Multiplication, Division, Addition, Subtraction) is used in math so that you can remember the order of operations. And of course we used the acronym "SMART" earlier on to help make the goal requirements more memorable.

Acrostics

Ideal for: Remembering a longer list (more than five things), or a series of ideas or names, like the countries on a map or the bones in the body.

An acrostic is an invented sentence or poem with first-letter cues that correspond to what you are trying to remember. For example, the order of the classifications of life is represented by the sentence, "Kings Play Cards On Fairly Good Soft Velvet." The first letter of each classification matches the first letter of each word to the first letter of each classification: Kings = Kingdom, Play = Phylum, Cards = Class, On = Order, Fairly = Family, Good = Genus, Soft = Species, Velvet = Variety. Note that the order of the words in the sentence matches the order of the words in the classification.

It can also help to divide that longer list into shorter sections. For example, when trying to remember the names and locations of countries on a map, divide the map up into sections of eight or fewer countries. Starting on the left side of the section and moving right, take the first letter of each country and then make a new sentence. This new sentence will help you remember the name and where each country is located.

Songs

Ideal for: Remembering a large amount of information.

For some people, learning song lyrics or creating a rhyme is much easier than memorizing a list. To do this, take what you are learning and put some music behind it. Take the words or list and put them to your favorite tune or add words to make a funny rhyme.

2. Flash cards

Flash cards are a portable and practical way of making information stick. One of the cool things about note cards is that the process of making them actually helps you to start learning the material. If you pay close attention as you go (rather than just copying things down and spacing out), you'll begin moving the information from your short-term memory into your permanent memory.

You can make note cards even more effective by using colored cards or colored dots. For example, if you are learning vocabulary and need to remember the parts of speech, designate separate colors for nouns, verbs, and adjectives. Then use the corresponding colored card or put a dot on the side of the card with the word to remind you which part of speech it is. That color will help you associate the word with the part of speech.

Flash cards are great for a self-quiz or for organizing information. They're individual and portable, so you can mix them up and regroup them. You can also make separate stacks of cards for words you know and words you don't know. Look at one side of the card and say the definition out loud (or name the term that's being defined). Flip it over and see if you got it right—then move on and repeat.

Practice (Tests) Make Perfect

As you learned in the section on memory, one of the most important aids to memory is repetition—or, to put it another way, practice. Tests are like a performance, like playing in the big game. If you want to do well when the spotlight is shining down on you, you have to make sure that you have it down cold when the pressure is off as well. The more you practice, and the better you do, the more confidence you'll gain as well. (And that confidence will serve you well when the clock starts ticking down and the pressure starts to build again.)

Tests can contain a wide variety of question styles, including multiple-choice, true/false, fill-in-the-blank, short and long essays, and problem-solving sections. If you do decide to take a practice test make sure that, you answer questions in the style that they are likely to appear on the actual exam. If you can bring in a sheet of notes to a history test, then you don't have to spend time memorizing a bunch of dates, and you can focus on more substantial issues instead. If you're not sure what to expect, use a combination of strategies so you'll be prepared for anything that comes your way.

The chart on the next page will help you figure out what kinds of responses are called for—and what kinds of studying tactics are required—for different kinds of tests.

Type of Test	How to demonstrate what you have learned	Ways to practice
• Short-answer questions • Essays • Location tests (e.g., identifying countries on a map) • Fill-in-the-blank • Oral exams	Recall: requires you to produce the answer from your memory without referring to any reference materials (notes, your book, etc.).	Talk it out Write it out Get quizzed
• Multiple-choice tests • Matching • True/false	Recognize: requires you to identify the correct answer from a list.	Get quizzed
• Short-answer questions • Essays • Problem sets (as in math, chemistry, or physics)	Application: requires you to take something you have learned and apply it to a new situation. This might include recalling information from memory.	Write it out Get quizzed

Practice Strategy #1: Talk It Out

One easy way to see whether or not you've really learned the material is to try and teach it to someone else. Find a friend from your class, a member of your study group, a parent, or even a potted plant, and start talking. Armed with your study tool, try and speak in terms that are clear and direct—in terms that even a potted plant would understand.

It's a good idea to focus on one section at a time, master it, and then move on to the next. It's okay to use your notes at first, but try to rely on them less and less as you go. After your first attempt, you will start to identify what information you've got down cold and what still needs a little work.

Practice Strategy #2: Write It Out

It's always a good idea to practice doing what you'll need to do on a test. For tests that require you to identify, locate, and name things, it's immensely helpful to write out samples ahead of time. For example, if you have to label a diagram, see if you can find a blank image, make copies, and then fill it in with the relevant information over and over again. For tests that require problem-solving, find some sample problems and get to work. Sometimes you might understand the material well enough when you read it over, but it can get more difficult when you're actually doing it on your own—without the aid of your notes or the book.

Practice Strategy #3: Get Quizzed

Another great way to make sure you have learned the material is to take practice tests. Finding practice tests can be tricky, because teachers don't always give them to you, but there are ways! If you've taken any quizzes in class, go back and review the questions and redo any problems you missed. Check your textbook and see if there are any end-of-chapter quizzes, unit reviews, or any other kind of assessments. For math or physics, look for problems in the textbook that you haven't done yet. Your textbook's website, if there is one, might also offer sample questions. Finally, make up your own test. Create sample questions from the headers in your textbook and then write out the answers.

And you can always use your study tool to quiz yourself, too! Just fold the paper over so that you can only see the main concepts, and start explaining! Or give the tool to a friend, parent, or sibling and ask them to ask you to explain the main ideas.

Chapter 11
Mastering the Test

On the day of the exam there are lots of things you can do to lower your anxiety and increase your chances of success. It's important to get in the right mindset—you want to feel relaxed and confident when you're taking the test. Get lots of rest the night before, and make sure you've eaten well. You want to have everything you need, like pencils, a calculator, note cards, etc. And whether it's multiple-choice, a true/false test, an essay exam, or a bunch of math problems, you want to bring your A-game so you can get down to business and take control of the test.

Bring Your A-Game

You've consolidated all your notes, taken a dozen practice tests, reviewed the material with your study group, and now it's show time. To be at your best, make sure you're physically and mentally prepared. This starts with a good night's sleep—ideally, nine hours. (This might be challenging, but the closer you can get to it, the better.) Research shows that sleep helps glue that new information into your mind. Without it, the information won't stick as well, even with all that studying. In addition to a good night's sleep, make sure that you have had a good meal beforehand, whether it's a hearty breakfast or lunch. And hit the bathroom *before* class.

Show up to your test a few minutes early so that you can settle in first. Take out what you need (pen, paper, water bottle, watch, calculator, etc.), steal one more glance at your study tool, and then just relax. Tests can be stressful, and taking a few moments before the exam to relax and get yourself in a positive mind set can make a huge difference.

TIME-SAVER: TEST KIT

Don't waste any precious test time looking for a pencil or pulling out the calculator. Put together a test kit and pack it with all the supplies you'll need:

- Sharp pencils

- Pens

- Erasers

- Calculator

- Binder paper

- Energy bar or snack (if it's okay with your teacher)

Get In the Zone

Top athletes perform at their best when they're in the "zone," that is, when their mind and body work in perfect harmony. You can apply this same concept to test performance. Here's how.

Step 1: Relax

The key to relaxation is breathing. Before the test begins, close your eyes and take a few deep, slow breaths. You'll begin to notice your whole body calming down. Your heart will beat more slowly, your palms will start to dry, and your mind will start to clear.

Step 2: Build confidence

Think about a time and place where you felt super confident and take a snapshot of that in your mind. Imagine yourself in that confident place as you continue your measured breathing.

Step 3: Take a positive attitude

Whether you like it or not, you have to take this test. As you open your eyes, gather all of that confidence and say something to yourself like, "I'm going to do really well on this test."

Manage the Test. Don't Let It Manage You

Students who perform well on tests don't just know their material—they also know how to manage their time. You'll need to use your planning and prioritization skills to get the best results. (So it's also a good idea to sit somewhere where you can see the clock.)

Dump information

As you take a couple of minutes in test preparation, try and unload some of what you'll need to refer to onto the test or a piece of paper. Whether it's a mnemonic device, a math formula, an organizational aid, or a quick list, jot it down quickly so that you don't have to worry about forgetting it later on.

Prioritize

As you go through the test, make sure that you spend the majority of your time accumulating as many points as possible. Spend more time on the sections that are worth more points. For example, if the true/false section is worth 10% of your grade, spend 10%

of your time—or less—in that section. Conversely, if the essay section is worth 50% of the test, make sure that you are giving yourself at least 50% of your time to work on it. The last thing you want to do is run out of time because you spent too much time on the section worth 10%!

Read the directions and questions carefully

There's nothing worse than writing two essays when you really only had to pick one of the two topics. Or selecting the wrong answer because you didn't read the word *not* in the question. You can easily avoid these frustrations by carefully reading directions and questions. If you're allowed to write on the test, be sure to underline or circle the key words. This will keep you focused on the right thing.

Do the easy questions first

Before you pick up your pen or pencil, scan the entire test to see how long it is, what types of questions are on it, and how many points each question or section is worth. That way, you can figure out what parts might be harder or easier for you and what parts are worth the most. Top test-takers regularly skip around the test to do the easiest questions first, tackle the most valuable questions next, skip over questions that they cannot answer right away, and go back through the test once they have finished to check their work.

If you have no clue how to solve or answer a question, skip it. But be sure to circle the number so that you can easily find it after you have completed the rest of the test. Sometimes as you go through the test there are clues in the other questions that help you to remember the answers to the ones you skipped!

Go with your gut

Your first instinct is usually right. It's when you think too hard that you convince yourself you're wrong. Unless you're super sure, default to your gut. You can always lightly mark your "gut" response and go back later for the final decision. And if you want to change your answer, be 100% sure that your initial answer was wrong.

Watch out for careless errors

Given that tests usually include time constraints and nerves, you are bound to make a careless error here and there. If you have time at the end of the test, go back over your answers. Check your math, and make sure that the right letter was bubbled or penciled in. Also, make sure you write your name on your test! (You'd be surprised at how easy it is to forget that step!)

Mastering the Multiple-Choice and True/False

Every test involves some element of strategizing, but this is especially true for multiple-choice and true/false tests. Both of these have only one right answer, and it's sitting right in front of you—you just need to identify it. Sometimes the answer is obvious, while at other times the test writer will include qualifying words or slight differences between answers, which can be very confusing. Use the resources below to give yourself the best possible chance, whatever the question may be.

Multiple-choice checklist

- ❑ Read the entire question and all answers carefully
- ❑ Underline key words or terms
- ❑ Cross out answers you know are not true

- ❑ Choose the answer that is most correct, and once you think you know the right answer, make sure the others are wrong. Usually the most complex, complete answer is correct.

- ❑ Be careful of negatives ("All of the following are true except . . .") —change the sentence into a positive so that it's easier to answer ("Which one of the following is false?")

- ❑ Make the best possible guess if you can only eliminate some of the answers

- ❑ If you have no idea, then just go with your gut

The Truth About True/False Tests

There are generally more true than false answers.

Even if you're not sure, you should always guess—unless there's a penalty. You have a 50% chance of getting each question right.

Words like *never*, *always*, and *every* mean that the statement must be true *all the time.*

Words like *usually*, *generally*, or *sometimes* mean that the statement may be true or false *depending on the circumstances.*

If any part of the statement is false, then the answer is false. However, if some part of a statement is true, it doesn't mean the entire statement is true.

The Essay Test

Essay questions can be extra challenging because they rely on both your writing skills and your ability to recall information. Plus, your time is limited, and you have to write out the answer by hand. Given these constraints, you will want to make sure that you understand the question and spend time organizing your thoughts so that you use your time wisely.

Read the directions and question carefully

Even if you previewed the question when you first got the test, make sure that you go back and carefully read the directions and question carefully. And then read it again! During the second read, underline or circle important words.

Organize your thoughts

Take everything you know about the topic you are writing about and jot it down. Some students prefer to make a list, while others like to show how words and concepts are related spatially. Either way is fine, just so long as you get everything you know down on paper. After that's done, put those ideas into a quick outline and you're ready to go.

Be clear

Make sure that it is really easy for the reader (aka your teacher) to understand your essay. Include a clear topic sentence and focus on one main idea per paragraph with several supporting details. If you make a mistake along the way, neatly cross it out rather than trying to erase it. This will take less time and look less sloppy in the long run.

Use your time wisely

While it's important to give yourself some thinking and prewriting time, you don't want to run out of actual writing time.

Try and spend no more than 20% of your allotted time organizing and thinking, leaving the majority of your time to write and review your essay. Spend the greatest amount of your writing time on your body paragraphs and less time on the introduction and conclusion. That being said, if a thesis statement is required, make sure it's clear and aligned with the rest of your answer.

Final Thoughts on Testing

No matter what type of test you're taking, it's important to remember that there's usually still more work to be done after the test is over (unless it's a final, of course). Take the time you need to step away and get your bearings again, but once you've received the test back and regained your composure, really take the time to examine your performance and reflect on what you've mastered, what you struggled with, and what you really don't understand at all. If you need help, ask for it; and if something just doesn't seem right—whether it's the overall grade or just a question that still doesn't make any sense, talk to your teacher about it. Do what you can to address the areas where you struggled so that when the next test comes along, you'll be likely to do better!

Conclusion

So now that you've finished reading, it's time to start actually incorporating these tips, tricks, and strategies into your everyday life! Because sure, you can read this book and memorize all the helpful hints—just like you can cram 200 years of European history into your brain the week before a final—but unless you start internalizing that advice, it's going to fade quickly into obscurity (along with all those dates you memorized for your last European history test...when was the French Revolution again...?).

But with that being said, it's also important to note that the suggestions and advice offered here should fit your life and your personality, and not the other way around. Don't worry too much about trying to fit yourself into the specific organizational and study methods that have been outlined here. Try the different techniques and see what works for you. You might want to just tweak some of the strategies, while others may have to be dropped entirely. Play around with these tactics, and make them your own. After all, the whole point is self-improvement—and you're the self that matters here. Play around with what you've learned and see what sticks.

And don't forget: The more organized you become, the more free time you'll have to enjoy the things in life you actually want to spend your time on, like friends, hobbies, and eating tacos. Go forth and conquer school! You can do it!

Index

About the Author

Lesley Schwartz Martin has been working in education for the last 15 years as a professional teen organizer, academic coach, classroom teacher, tutor, and product designer. She started working with teens as a high school social studies teacher in the Bay Area. After leaving the classroom, she combined her experiences as an educator with her skills as an organizer to help teach young students how to managetheir time and keep their school lives in order. Additionally, she founded ClassTracker (www.classtracker.com), a company that creates customized academic planners for middle and high schools. Lesley lives with her family in San Francisco, California.

Acknowledgements

Tremendous thanks to my husband for his support, love, encouragement, and all the ways that he picked up the pieces while I worked on the book. I'm also grateful to my parents for teaching me most of what I know about getting and staying organized. Finally, I want to thank all my former students— without whom all of this would be just theory.

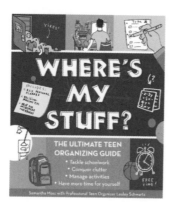

More Zest Books on School Life

For more tips and tricks on how to organize your schedule, locker, backpack, and more, check out ·Where's My Stuff?: The Ultimate Teen Organizing Guide

Free time is great. Unless you spend all of it searching for your home-work, your cell phone, or a clean pair of gym shorts. Then free time is not so great. In fact, it's nonexistent. If chaos and disorganization are swallowing all of your free time, Where's My Stuff? can help you get it back.

Inside, you'll learn how to systematically organize your school stuff, your time, and your room. Where's My Stuff? includes:

• innovative notebook systems

• backpack maintenance tips

• practical pointers for managing your schedule

• a template for your own personalized daily planner

• interior design-inspired techniques to make your room your fave place to be

With fun and useful illustrations, easy-to-follow charts, and ample doses of humor, Where's My Stuff? is an incredible asset for anyone who wants to getit together ... and keep it together, for good.

Visit www.zestbooks.net/wheres-my-stuff/ to order your copy of Where's My Stuff?: The Ultimate Teen Organizing Guide today!

These Zest Books are available wherever books are sold or at www.zestbooks.net.